THE HEART OF CRICKET

TOM GRAVENEY

THE HEART OF CRICKET

Arthur Barker Limited   London
A subsidiary of Weidenfeld (Publishers) Limited

Printed in Great Britain by
Butler & Tanner Ltd
Frome and London

Contents

Illustrations

1
Into County Cricket — by Accident

Fate, I am convinced, is a confirmed, irresponsible, two-timing jester.

How else can I explain the happy accidents of my entry into first-class cricket – almost as if an inviting door had been casually opened – and to the BBC as a television pundit?

Or, on the reverse side of the coin, the blockbusting distress caused to me and my family when I departed the Test scene under the cloud of censure and suspension. Me, Thomas William Graveney, OBE (and, mark you, awarded while I was still playing), a loyalist to my finger tips, virtually being accused of putting my benefit before England's interests! I still have to pinch myself to believe it really happened.

There was the pride-wounding, almost laughable saga of losing the Gloucestershire captaincy to an untried amateur, with the undertones of an alleged players' revolt. Two players don't even constitute a quorum! Also there remains a lasting suspicion that I sacrificed my prospects of becoming England's appointed captain for blowing my top off to a high-ranking Pakistani official while standing up on behalf of my frightened team-mates – yes, physically frightened – and missed a tour to South Africa, the only Test-playing country I did not visit, because of an innocent handshake.

For a character generally portrayed as affable, easy-going, golf-loving and as outwardly placid as my adopted Cotswolds, I certainly had my squalls and moments of choppy waters. Twice in Test matches, at Lords against Australia and at Barbados, my captain, Sir Len Hutton, who, I suspect, dismissed my batting technique as too flashy, restrained me as I was slipping into top gear, with unforgettable results. I was at the centre of a row at Port-of-Spain when I threw the ball to the ground, more through frustration and despair than through anger, after completing the simplest of slip catches which, astonishingly, was disallowed – a last-straw incident for the entire England side.

Normally I did not resent what was written about me, and I soon developed a simple philosophy. As I didn't need the newspapers to tell me I had played a bad innings, I simply did not read them when things did not go right. I was, however, upset when one of the so-called 'heavies' made out that my journey to Luton to play in my benefit match on the Sunday, the rest day, of the Old Trafford Test in 1969 was made 'in a fit of pique at not being made captain'. A solicitor friend suggested taking legal action as he considered the comment defamatory. I preferred a dignified silence.

On the whole, however, my relationship with the media was friendly and, since I have had some experience both in writing and commentating, I realise the difficulty of maintaining an acceptable standard day by day. The wise sportsman soon learns that praise and criticism are both impostors, a matter of swings and roundabouts, and certainly nothing to get a complex about.

Because I strayed into professional cricket by mistake, I had almost none of the orthodox apprenticeship of the county player. While my England colleagues like Sir Len Hutton, Denis Compton, Peter May, Colin Cowdrey and Co. were carefully groomed either on ground staffs or through public school and University, my earliest post-schooldays were spent as a young soldier bent on the military life. In some ways, I suppose, my background fashioned an independence of thought which, for good or bad, never deserted me. If I hadn't enjoyed playing, travel to distant lands, and the ever-present challenges, I would not have carried on – though, admittedly, I had some wretched low points. My batting philosophy remained basically the same, despite some attempts to change it, and it would have been anathema for me to grind out runs in the Geoff Boycott, Chris Tavaré fashion. To me the way a batsman gets his runs is almost as important as the style of life itself.

I joined the Army at seventeen, straight from Bristol Grammar School, and I spent six months doing basic training at a Young Soldiers Battalion. The next stage was pre-OCTU, then OCTU, after which I duly became 2nd Lieut. T.W. Graveney 364610 of the Gloucestershire Regiment with a posting to the Middle East. While waiting to join my Regiment, 2/4 Hampshires, I spent three weeks at a transit camp at Cairo, where I managed some cricket and, to my surprise, quite a few runs. From Cairo I moved on to Greece and more cricket on a rough coir matting, which, to prove that no experience is entirely valueless, was to stand me in good stead when I went to India and the West Indies with MCC. (Port-of-Spain, at the time, had jute matting. Some will have it that matting is the fairest of all cricket pitches and guarantees play without interruptions. On Hutton's tour in 1953–54, there was a curious exception to this theory, for a damp patch had been left where the clay-sand base under the mat had been rolled and watered overnight. England's innings resumed forty-three minutes late!)

In Greece the Brigade broke up, and I was posted to the 28th Field Regiment, Royal Artillery, with 25-pounders. The Regiment was posted back to Egypt, and I was asked if I wanted to stay in the Artillery. My answer was no, because I had been originally commissioned with the Gloucesters and I had kept their badge up. 'Right,' was the response, 'You'd better find yourself a job somewhere else.' Please bear with me, because the postings were leading me tortuously to the cricket field, and eventually to the England side.

Back I went to the transit camp, now at Suez, and the G3 took one look at me and exclaimed, 'You're the chap who was in Cairo and scored a lot of runs. How would you like to stay as Sports Officer at the transit depot?' Here, indeed, was a job to suit my catholic sporting tastes. I played everything – cricket, soccer, rugby, golf, basketball, tennis, hockey, athletics – the lot.

I stayed at the depot until I was due for a month's leave. By that time, Ken, my elder brother, who had been commissioned in the 41st Royal Marine Commandos and could not settle in his office boy job with Shell, Bristol, had decided to have a go at first-class cricket. He had done well with Gloucestershire as a fast-medium bowler and hard-hitting left-hand batsman. The county had narrowly lost the 1947 county championship after a thrilling decider with Middlesex at Cheltenham, and Ken, who was to take all-ten wickets in an innings and in time become the club's chairman, was hooked on the life.

Charlie Barnett, one of the most attractive and punishing opening batsmen it has been my good fortune to see, was having his benefit in 1947, and Ken said he had a brother able to make the number up if he was short for the exhibition matches with the clubs and villages. Ken's recommendation was: 'He's not a bad cricketer.'

The upshot was that I not only played but opened the innings, usually with Alfie Wilcox, a member of the Gloucestershire staff, for the simple reason that the senior players on such occasions preferred to bat lower down for a slog to entertain the crowd. I must have done well enough to impress Charlie, for he soon arranged a more testing trial for me.

Five of Essex's team were included in a Stinchcombe XI and the opening bowlers were given a new ball to use against me. My partner was the late Billy Neale, a county stalwart, and after I had scored thirty-odd runs reasonably well I was asked what I intended to do when I left the Army. As there had been hints of my becoming a staff officer in physical training – an attractive proposition at the age of twenty – I said the Army was to be my future. But, in the end, the call of cricket was all-powerful.

One powerful reason for my change of mind was that I had

enjoyed myself immensely playing with the Gloucestershire boys. It was almost like being received into a delightful free-masonry. The happy accident. I was slightly, and rightly, in awe of the seniors like Charlie Barnett, George Emmett, Jack Crapp and Tom Goddard, but they could not have been more helpful in my development. There was the inevitable ribbing when, as Emmett's partner, I collected a 'duck' in my first innings at Oxford. 'Well, you can only get better' was the playful comment.

Behind the banter and the leg-pulling was the unobtrusive but important help of the senior batsmen, who would act like willing schoolmasters coaching a pupil. If there was a problem with a bowler I had not faced, I would be briefed. For instance when I played against Doug Wright his fast leg-spin and googlies were quite enough to contend with, let alone his kangaroo hop to the wicket. Jack Crapp was my partner and he contrived to shield me from Wright. I soon realised the old-style pro was the salt of the earth.

My demob had taken from the end of January 1948, and until I reported at the Bristol headquarters on 1 April – a date I figured not inappropriate in my struggling early days – I played golf and generally amused myself. The oft-repeated story that I had the choice between cricket and golf as a profession is flattering but not strictly accurate, though golf is a passion and, at my peak, I had a handicap of one, compared with six today. I had my first handicap while still at school during the war and aged fifteen. I asked the secretary at Henbury Golf Club near Bristol: 'Please, sir, can I have a handicap?' He asked what I usually went around in. 'Oh, about 80,' I said. 'All right, your handicap is 8' he said.

There were times when it was said my golf interfered with my cricket, but that was so much nonsense. To go on the links on tour was the perfect relaxation. Sir Don Bradman, captain of the unbeatable Australians of 1948, actually recommended golf to his players when they were not required for cricket. I thought what was good enough for Bradman was good enough for Graveney.

My family had moved from Riding Mill, Northumberland, where I was born, to Bristol, via Fleetwood, after the death of my father when I was six. I was the middle of five children – I had an elder brother and sister and a younger brother and sister – and my mother remarried. Bob Gardner, a cousin of the family, became my step-father. He was with Sir Lindsay Parkinson, the Wimpeys of the North, and was working at Leyland, Lancashire. After I had started at Arnold House School, Blackpool, he was sent to a building project at Avonmouth docks in 1938, and I went to Bristol Grammar School.

I have lived in Gloucestershire ever since, and once I had scored a couple of runs for the county the West Country were ready to accept me as one of their own! Of course I regard myself as much a part of this delectable corner of England as Clifton Bridge. I now live in a house of stout Cotswold stone which was once a stable, and I believe my adoption to be complete.

Not many aspiring young players had a worse start than me. Not daring to work out the actual figure, I hazard a guess my first twenty-five innings produced no more than two hundred runs. The reason was simple: the bowling was different, far better and more accurate than I had encountered before, and I knew only too well there was a lot to learn if I was to make the grade. Progress, if any, was like an erratic ride on a switchback, for although I was able to score heavily in the Second XI, as soon as I was restored to the championship team I would fall with a thump. My twenty-first birthday present was to be dropped, but then Billy Neale pulled a hamstring so badly that he was out of action for some time.

As the professional staff numbered only thirteen, and George Emmett and Jack Crapp were chosen to play in the Old Trafford Test against Australia, Gloucestershire had no alternative but to go back to me. I can well imagine the resigned reluctance of the county selectors when I was despatched to Bournemouth, but an innings of 47 on a turning pitch against the notable spinners Jim Bailey and Charlie Knott restored my fortunes. Although I managed only a single in the second innings, I scarcely looked back from that breakthrough on a turning pitch.

In the following game against Somerset at Bristol I was 81 at declaration, and, in the month of August my maiden first-class century came off Combined Services at Gloucester, after a first innings of 89. No one forgets his first hundred and I am no exception, and so, after initial disappointments, I ended the season with a vindicated faith that I would get there in the end. *Wisden* recorded: 'A pleasant feature [of the season] was the form of a newcomer, T.W. Graveney, a product of Bristol club cricket, who showed graceful right-handed stroke play.' If I had not enjoyed that successful August no doubt my attitude for my second season would have been one of apprehension and vastly different. I am always sorry for the young player who tantalisingly fails to bridge that important gap between first and second XI county cricket.

True to form, my Test beginnings were also something of a mistake. South Africa were the visitors in 1951 and I was called up for the third Test at Old Trafford as a stand-by for Denis Compton who had done something unusual for him by missing a full toss which landed on a toe. Denis failed to survive his fitness test, and I had my baptism in Test cricket on a sticky wicket. My contribution was a modest 15, but 15 on a wicket with the ball jumping around like a demented thing was worth many a 50 on another day. I was bowled by the off-spinner Athol Rowan, whose first ball to Len Hutton, as he leant forward, turned, lifted and hit him on his shoulder.

The match was a new experience for me. I not only saw Alec Bedser bowling almost unplayable leg-cutters and have match figures of 12 for 112, but a side of international cricket I would never have dreamed possible.

It centred on Hutton, who was one short of his hundredth first-class century. At that time no batsman had ever completed the feat in a Test, although Geoff Boycott was later to do so against Australia, and on his home ground at Headingley.

England had to get 139 to win, and because of rain play did not start until an hour before the close on the fourth evening. The wicket was soaked, kicking and lifting nastily, and Cuan McCarthy, the big fast bowler, had a half-gale at his back. I sat on the players' balcony with a silent prayer that I would be spared another trial at least not that evening. Fortunately, McCarthy did not have the nous to pitch the ball up and, indeed, he was often so short that the ball flew over the batsmen. Nevertheless, it was a severe physical ordeal for Hutton and Jack Ikin, who was absolutely black and blue with bruising on his chest and arms – the penalty of taking the brunt of the fire and bravely getting behind the ball. You couldn't do other than admire the wily old fox Hutton, who adroitly managed always to take a single off McCarthy at the appropriate time. Just before the close Len was hit on the pads by McCarthy and he went down as if hit by a sniper. And there he stayed until we in the dressing-room reckoned it had cost South Africa two overs.

Though the wicket had eased the next morning a huge, slowly approaching black cloud menaced England and, instead of going in whack, whack and winning before it shed its rain-load first Ikin and then Reg Simpson blocked to allow Len to get most of the runs and draw closer to his century. I scratched my head and wondered whether all the stories I had been told about Test cricket were fantasies. Here they were playing it for fun! It did rain, but during lunch when Hutton was 91 and England were four short of winning.

Afterwards I watched with fascination as Len added three more off McCarthy, thus getting the strike. He then needed a six to reach his century and the slow left-arm spinner, the late 'Tufty' Mann, bowled a slow full-toss with an obvious message to be hit. But Len contrived to get a bit of a bottom corner on it and the ball went high over square-leg, falling short of the boundary for four. Soon after Len scored his hundredth century at The Oval against Surrey, and *Wisden* commented: 'Records which arrive naturally are more commendable than those which are sought.'

2
A Scalding Start in Television

Out of the blue one day in 1979 came a telephone call from
Christopher Martin-Jenkins, broadcaster, Editor of the
Cricketer International and the 'Mike Yarwood' of cricket
dinners with his gifted impressions. Christopher had a pro-
posal to put to me. As India had four Tests with England
after the Prudential Cup would I, as a former tourist of the
sub-continent, give a general talk on Indian cricket for the
BBC? I had toured India, Pakistan and Ceylon (now Sri
Lanka) in 1951-52, and needed no second bidding. A first
tour always leaves a lasting impression, and, it can be truth-
fully said, India before European-style hotels and cuisines,
with its heat, dust, crowds and exotic customs, was always an
unforgettable experience.

A mischievous thought crossed my mind as soon as the
invitation was made: 'Heavens, am I the only living survivor?'
But I thought it would be a congenial one-off job talking over
old times. Not for one fleeting second did it occur to me that
a casual call was to prove another happy accident which
would change the course of my life.

Since my playing days I had hankered for a chance to
return to the game in some capacity or other. Umpiring was
not for me, and the little coaching I did at Dean Close School,
Cheltenham, while I had a pub close to the racecourse, did
not fulfil my need. Rather to my surprise I missed the game,
the camaraderie, the banter with officials and members of the

media, the deep inner satisfaction of a well-played innings – even perhaps the glamour of being a sporting figure – more than I had imagined possible. And it is one of those human foibles that the moment a cricketer stops playing, he is twice the player! As with Army service, the good times are affectionately remembered; the bad mercifully forgotten.

It hurt like hell to be out of things, and, strangely, most of all when I was behind the bar, when all around me the talk was of sport – often of cricket and cricketers past and present. Memories flooded back, and a wall of loneliness seemed to encompass me. I realised I was no more part of the game than the chaps in cheerful argument on the other side of the counter.

Jackie, my wife, with feminine intuition, sensed what was wrong. 'What a waste to have someone like you behind the bar when you should be passing on your experience and knowledge to others,' she said. She persuaded me to write to Richie Benaud to see if there were any opportunities in radio or broadcasting; but there had been no vacancies at the time.

I went up to London to record my talk for the BBC. Obviously there was a lot bottled up inside me, waiting to come out, for I did not stop talking for almost an hour. The words gushed out, time was forgotten, and I moved from India to cover what must have been the entire spectrum of the modern game. When Christopher played back the tape it sounded reasonably well, and we retired to the BBC Club for a drink. Shortly we were joined by Peter Baxter, producer in charge of cricket on radio. Baxter asked me if I had ever thought of doing cricket commentaries. 'I have thought about it,' I replied, 'but no one has ever asked me.'

My timing with my appearance at the BBC must have been better than on those occasions when I struggled to find my touch at the crease. Baxter went on to say that with the World Cup ahead he was short of commentators. He added: 'There are big matches in different parts of the country on the same day. Would you like to have a go?'

Well, there was only one answer to that, and I became one

of the 'experts' supporting Freddie Trueman and Trevor Bailey. My other companions were the incomparable John Arlott, now retired, and Don Mosey, the forthright northerner. Not knowing the ropes, I was more nervous than before my first Test innings.

I was fortunate both in my colleagues, who did everything to help, and in that I was allocated exciting matches. One was the high-scoring semi-final between the West Indies and Pakistan at the Oval. I could hardly have failed. The crowd of 20,000 ensured an electric atmosphere, and batsmen like Gordon Greenidge, Viv Richards, Clive Lloyd, Majid Khan and Zaheer Abbas adorned the match with glorious attacking shots. The Pakistan pair took 166 off thirty-six overs, but the West Indies, who were unbeatable in the first two Prudential Cups, won by 43 runs. I hate to think what my fate might have been if it had been one of those awful days of defensive attrition with overs slowly bowled and a plethora of short-pitched bowling – days which, alas, have been all too common in five-day matches.

While I was at a game at Edgbaston I met the television people, and shortly afterwards I had a call from Jim Laker to tell me the producer was on the look-out for someone to supplement his team. Again I was asked if I would like to have a go. And that's how it all happened ... a very fortunate break which has enabled me to get back into the game.

My luck continued in the third Test at Headingley when Ian Botham hit India's bowling all over the ground and missed a century before lunch by just one run – a marvellous innings by a fine player – and exciting television. No commentator could fail to respond, and I was gradually given more time, primarily for what might be termed the 'inter-round summaries' made famous on radio boxing by the late Barrington Dalby.

I literally had the hottest of receptions on television. You are given a pair of 'cans' to put over your ears, a lip microphone is set in front of you, and, for better or worse, you take it from there. You listen intently to the previous commentator

– in my first instance Ted Dexter – and start talking, being careful to maintain the general drift of the comments.

Then came my big moment. Here I was about to stamp my personality and authority on the great, unsuspecting British public. Just as I was about to take the microphone an assistant studio manager upset a scalding cup of coffee over my arm. By the grace of some guardian angel watching over me, I instinctively pushed the microphone down and by the barest possible margin my painful expletive escaped being picked up. Had it come across I fear my first word, though sensational, would have proved my last, and I might have made it into the *Guinness Book of Records* heading a column under the title: Brief Television Appearances.

I can laugh about it now, but at the time it was no joke. I was in severe pain and I had to go, hot-foot and hot-armed, to the England dressing-room for first-aid treatment.

The scalding apart, I could not have wished for more help than I had from the old pros Peter West, Richie Benaud, Jim Laker and Co., and the two main producers, Nick Hunter and Bill Taylor. All were first-class companions, ever ready to help and ease me into my new role. Richie set me up when he said: 'If you want to say something just give me a nudge and I'll bring you in and introduce you. The best thing you can do is talk just as if you are talking to me. If you do it like that you'll come over naturally. You'll not be uptight. Naturalness is what commentating is all about.'

That was probably the best advice I could have had. Nothing is worse on television than insincerity or striving to be other than your natural self. The camera devastatingly unmasks the sham.

As time went on, the greater became my admiration for Peter West, the link man and the ultimate in professionalism. Having watched him over the years as presenter for cricket and other sports, and not forgetting the suave master of ceremonies in *Come Dancing*, I suppose, like most viewers, I took him for granted. As a player I reckoned anyone could do his job, and that he was a bit of a smoothie. I had never appreciated the difficulty of some of the things he is called upon to do: things like introducing the programme cold; setting up the scene with the weather, the state of the game and the pitch; recalling the highlights of the previous day's play, and so on. Without a polished and yet factual précis there would be no start and stuffing to the programme, and, like an accomplished actor or writer, he makes it all seem so easy. In fact his job can be far from easy.

Like all the television pros Peter has an ear mike to connect him with the producer, and while Peter is talking to the viewers the producer is talking to him. A fair comparison might be to use the phone and carry on a conversation with someone else at the same time. Occasionally during our summaries I have noticed Peter's eyes glaze for a split second as he has switched off the half of his mind connected to Graveney and concentrated on an urgent voice in his ear. Only a very able and practised performer could hope to do two things at once in front of millions of eyes, but if I detect a fleeting blank look I know he has not heard everything I have said, and I take appropriate action, usually by talking a few seconds longer. Even so he has never totally lost the thread of our question-and-answer session, and never appears to be other than relaxed and at ease.

Only once have I seen him rattled, and that was when he was the victim of a practical joke on his birthday during a Test between England and Pakistan in 1982. Nick Hunter arranged for a singing telegram to be delivered, and we had all been made conspirators in the plot. Peter had closed the programme when Nick said: 'Pakistan TV have asked for a little chat between yourself, Richie and Jim about the comparison of the team that's here now and those that have been here before.' Peter began in the interview room, with lights blazing, cameras turning – the lot – and was in the middle of his expert analysis when suddenly a girl dressed as a Hawaian Hula Hula dancer appeared and began to sing 'Happy Birthday to you, Happy Birthday dear Peter, Happy Birthday to you.'

Until the penny dropped and he realised he had been conned, the look on his face defied description. No doubt he had visions of hitting the front pages of next morning's newspapers.

Television and radio, like most things, are a matter of teamwork, and the styles of Richie Benaud and Jim Laker, though as different as the men themselves, blend and complement each other perfectly. Benaud's reputation is richly deserved. He has taken to television the same direct, no-nonsense approach which made him such a powerful leader. When he became captain of Australia there were fears that, as an all-rounder, he already had too much on his plate. Those misgivings were quickly dispelled, as clearly he relished responsibility. What was not anticipated to the full was his deep tactical knowledge. Moreover he had the courage to put his theories to the test. With his cricket background and journalistic training Richie was ideally equipped for his career in television. He says what he thinks without causing offence. He has the vocabulary and the articulateness to go to the heart of the subject at hand, whether during the course of play, or in post-play analysis. Nothing escapes him, whether important or seemingly trivial, and he is never short of the right word. He is scrupulously fair, and even when, as a good Aussie, his heart must have been bleeding when England came back from the dead in 1981, he never yielded to disappointment or bias. There were some who regretted his past link with Kerry Packer, but that is another story, another argument, and all I will say is that had he gone television would have been immeasurably the poorer by the loss of his impressive presence.

There can be no one whose opinion commands more respect. His subjective, dispassionate examinations of the umpiring decisions during the 1982 games in England was masterly.

Jim Laker's habit of dropping his 'g's at the end of a word has been pounced on by the elocution purists, but it goes without saying he is a genuine authority and his droll northern humour unfailingly comes out. Jim never attempts to paint an elaborate picture; indeed as a television commentator he is not required to do so. If his language is plain and factual, he informs and guides in a manner which those with a cricket background especially appreciate.

Television, with events unfolding before the viewers, demands more discipline from its commentators than radio. The temptation to talk too much is strong for the beginner. Viewers do not need to be told what they can see for themselves, and the art is to observe and inform without being over-technical. Stating the obvious and the overworked cliché can be irritating. The close-ups give the armchair spectator an insight denied even to those with the best seats on the ground.

I have heard television berated because of the replays of dismissals and the instant examination of umpires' decisions. The truth, I think, is that more often than not, umpires are shown to be right. If anything, television has provided certain proof of the generally high standard of umpiring in England, and that some of the loudest and most fervent appeals are spurious. Of course television, being two-dimensional, is not infallible and decisions must still be left to the judgment of the umpire, which is a fundamental reason why I do not believe in a future of instant play-backs on a huge screen. If the game, already deprived of some of its individuality by helmets and the rest, is to be dehumanised to that extent, it should be played by robots.

The cameras have also put all-seeing eyes on the behaviour of players and crowds. I recall times when I returned from abroad to find the public highly sceptical of riots and incidents on the field. Local officials were wont to cry that it was all highly exaggerated. After a little interval even the Georgetown riot of 1953-4 – when bottles and other objects were hurled onto the pitch following a run-out – was played down as the invention of the 'foreign' correspondents. No longer can authority hide behind a smokescreen of denials.

Undeniably television has also brought its problems to

cricket. More would-be customers stay at home and watch Tests on the screen. The game itself finds competitiors once undreamed of in snooker, show jumping, soccer in mid-summer and so on. I wonder if it could be worked out how much it would cost in the course of a year to attend all the major sports from all over the world available on the screen? Only the very rich could afford the expense of tickets, travel, hotel and incidentals. Now cable television is in the offing – one channel with nothing but sport. It may be that basketball, American gridiron football and the like, all well subsidised, will further knock the ancient game of cricket. In a matter of a few generations the sporting habits of a nation have changed, all because of the little box.

Initially radio did a lot for cricket, bringing the personalities of the day and interest into countless homes. That radio still has its adherents is largely due to pioneers of the calibre of Howard Marshall, the unique descriptive powers of John Arlott and the ready wit of Brian Johnston, who, thankfully, has never grown up to stuffy old age. Johnston was a practical joker at Oxford, and has been prominent in the well-known programmes *In Town Tonight* and *Down Your Way* – and, if you can't take a joke, he's a positive danger to have around. He loves his cricket and cricketers, and life itself, and he is a guarantee that cricket radio is never sombre or too self-satisfied. There is sometimes an air of banter, as jokes and quips are exchanged, corks pop and cakes sent by listeners are ceremoniously cut. But the occasional irrelevance of the office party atmosphere does not impair the overall standard of expert commentary, though John Arlott, now retired, is sadly missed. It is impossible to replace an original.

Sitting alongside John in the commentary box I marvelled at his descriptive genius, and the word pictures he painted in that slow, deliberate Hampshire burr – almost an echo down the centuries of the Hambledon players. His voice was accepted as the voice of cricket in every English-speaking corner of the world, and he was a supremely gifted broadcaster.

John was touched heavily by personal tragedy, but his humour and philosophies never deserted him. His many interests include the collection of antiques and old books. He loves beautiful things – words for instance – and he is a connoisseur of wine. Lunch seemed to be an occasion to him rather than a break from duty. After one rather lavish entertainment on a rainy day at The Oval he retired to the press box. When he was awakened with the disturbing news that play was re-starting, he said, 'Oh dear, I lunched for no play today.' He was still able to pen his usual admirable piece for the *Guardian*.

3
Sacked by Gloucestershire and England

For a chap with the reputation (or flaw) of being easy-going, I have had some surprising upsets and brushes with authority. Not the least hurtful was to be sacked in 1961 from the captaincy of Gloucestershire after two years, without even the minor consolation of regaining my previous position as senior pro. Maybe during the machinations which led to Tom Pugh, an Old Etonian amateur, taking over, it was said, 'Tom won't mind.' As it turned out, Arthur Milton, my close friend and a regular golfing companion, was to be Pugh's right-hand man and senior pro.

Pugh had been recommended to the county by Percy Fender, the former Surrey and England all-rounder, as 'another Dexter'. As I had spent most of my two seasons trying to keep Pugh out of the championship side because I did not think he was up to scratch, I can only assume the once famous judgment of a legendary Surrey captain had declined over the years. Tom had the pedigree, but not the class of a county batsman, and in 1961 he missed eighteen matches after being lbw to a full toss from Northamptonshire's David Larter. Pugh though Larter was going to bowl a bumper, and ducked into a ball which never hit the ground.

Later Pugh, who was apologetic and embarrassed by the furore his appointment caused, informed me during a round of golf at Frilford Heath that Gloucestershire had told him two years previously that he was to have the captaincy. In other words I was destined for the chop from the day I took over in 1959 after my return from Peter May's disastrous tour of throwing and dragging in Australia.

The events leading to my dismissal left me dismayed. Gloucestershire announced that they had lost £15,000 in the season, a tidy sum in 1960, and that there was to be a change of captains. I took a dim view of that, for it was rather as if the captain was to blame for the loss. The fact is that, with the majority of home matches played at Bristol, Gloucestershire have little chance of breaking even, let alone making a profit. Bristol, a city of over half a million inhabitants, is astonishingly apathetic in its support of cricket. But for its membership, and the scheme my brother Ken set up with Phoenix Insurance when he was chairman, the club would either go under or have to find new headquarters.

An example of the county's indifference occurred during my first season, when Gloucestershire were at home to Essex in the Cheltenham Festival. At a function a civic dignitary prefaced his remarks with an apology for the performances of the side so far in the match. He then plunged into deeper waters.

'However, I extend a warm welcome to our visitors from Exeter, and to the home side, particularly to Tom Gravity and his brother Ken.' Doug Insole has called me 'Gravity' ever since.

Though I had, without exaggeration, hundreds of letters from members urging me to stay, the club's attitude, which suggested they did not care over much either way, was a strong reason for my final decision to leave. It was not that Gloucestershire had done badly on the field, and the rumour that there had been a 'dressing-room revolt' was so much nonsense. If there was dissatisfaction it came from a tiny minority – not more than two players. There was no trouble in the camp.

In my first season as skipper Gloucestershire were runners-up and were praised by *Wisden* as 'an attractive side to watch'. The previous year they were fourteenth, and, if a different pitch had been prepared for the crucial late-August fixture with Surrey at Gloucester, I might have led the champions. Gloucestershire learned the painful truth that the home side should not offer a turning and lifting pitch to opponents including Tony Lock and Jim Laker. Between them they shared all nineteen wickets to fall to bowlers, and they bowled all but four overs in the two Gloucestershire innings. The fact was that, in the context of the championship situation, Gloucestershire had to get a result, and to their misfortune it went the wrong way.

Yorkshire, the eventual champions, were dismissed for 35 at Bristol, only Brian Bolus reaching double figures and the last six batsmen collecting 'ducks' as Tony Brown took 7 for 11. The next season was far less successful, with a drop to eighth position, but the side were plagued with injuries. I had a shoulder muscle which worried me deep into the summer, and Arthur Milton was unable to play after June as he fractured a finger in our 3-wicket victory over the South Africans. The touring side were out for 49 in their second innings.

Other counties, Glamorgan, Warwickshire, Surrey and Hampshire, also dived in the table, but, apart from Wilf Wooller, all their captains were retained. But, of course, my fate had long been pre-ordained. The promise that he would be made captain was one of the reasons for Tom Pugh joining Gloucestershire.

Maybe I had my faults as a captain. Not that it was easy handling an attack consisting of two medium pacers, Tony Brown and David Smith, both of whom bowled off short runs, first-class spinners, David Allen, John Mortimore and 'Bomber' Wells – Allen and Mortimore were England bowlers – and Sam Cook, slow left-arm. Inevitably it took some sorting out who was to have first crack among the spinners, and I began working on the principle that the first chance went to the best bowler of the previous game. The theorist might scorn such a practice, but it was a method and worked reasonably well. Also, without a fast bowler, Gloucestershire raced through their overs with exemplary speed, but to the decided advantage of opposition batsmen, who received more deliveries per hour than they dared to expect. A standard performance was eighty-five overs completed by 3.45 p.m. if we fielded on the first day, and there was nothing the captain could do to alter the situation. Len Hutton would have been driven to distraction.

When the news was broken to me that I was to be deposed, the future appeared black enough to make me think of leaving first-class cricket. The prospect of an international comeback after a two-year absence seemed too far-fetched to warrant serious thought – how wrong that turned out to be – and there was apparently nothing left for me with Gloucestershire. On reflection, I am sure the absence of the secretary Howard Thomas, in hospital having an operation, was a misfortune both to the club and myself. There were plenty of senior officers on the bridge, but no hand on the tiller.

I became increasingly surprised and disenchanted by the sequence of events, and by the all too obvious fact that nobody seemed to care whether I remained with the club or not. Almost alone Ken did his best to persuade me to hold fast and change my mind. The President, the Duke of Beaufort, a lovely man if ever there was one, was apparently among those surprised by the committee's decision to replace me, and one evening there was a meeting at Badminton designed to clear the air. Present were the Duke, Sir William Grant (the Chairman), Sir Percy Lister (Vice-Chairman), my ever-faithful Ken, who had a one hundred per cent attendance record at all the meetings, and myself.

The sequel was that by the end of the evening I had agreed to continue to play for the county at the same salary. The club, in turn, gave an undertaking to find me a job in industry, to reinstate me as senior pro, and to guarantee I would not lose financially – the latter condition was to be a halter around my neck as it effectively tied me to the county. When I asked for the assurance to be put in writing, I was told to expect a letter within three or four days. I am still waiting for it.

I have to admit that deep down I did not want to continue playing for Gloucestershire. My pride was bruised, and as facts were uncovered it was all too evident that I was cast in the role of the fall-guy. My appointment in the first place had been a holding operation – to keep the seat warm for Pugh. Yet I was prepared to sink all differences, and to do so I had gone all the way with the club. As the weeks dragged on, however, and the promised letter did not arrive, I was resolved to quit first-class cricket and find a job outside the game. There seemed no other alternative.

Finally, with no one except my brother directly involved with the club seeming to care, I resigned.

Sir George Dowty, a captain of industry and a member of both Gloucestershire and Worcestershire committees, persuaded me to join Worcestershire. I was heartened to read in the newspapers that Gloucestershire accepted my full release and wished me luck in the future, but as the only consistent thing about them was inconsistency, I half-expected an objection to my registration with a new county. It duly happened and, though it might appear as a negation of natural justice, Gloucestershire were able to do so within the regulations, as they had offered me the same financial terms.

I think I speak for the vast majority in county cricket, and not least the players, when I say that a transfer system on soccer lines would be unwelcome and undesirable. The objections are obvious: a cornering of the best players by the better-off counties, under-cover payments, trumped-up differences between player and club as an excuse to move on for better terms, and a growth industry of shadowy agents. As it is there are whispered complaints already of young players being approached allegedly by third parties who, if unmasked, are disowned by the offending clubs.

Moreover it is true that county cricket's better relationships have been built on loyalty and mutual trust between club and players. Often in the past players did not bother to sign their contracts!

But I suggest there is more than a whiff of serfdom about

the position which leaves the employer holding the trump card as long as he doesn't cut his employee's wages, and, in my case he was clearly at fault in not fulfilling a verbal promise to put it in black and white. It is not to be wondered at that the authorities are now terrified by threats of legal action, and I doubt whether nowadays I would have been required to spend a year qualifying for Worcestershire, which meant I could not play in the county championship. My arguments were eloquently put to the sub-committee, chaired by Lord Cornwallis of the then Advisory County Cricket Committee, by Ryder Richardson, QC, the Recorder of Stoke and a friend of a member of the Worcestershire Committee, but to no avail.

As Alex Bannister commented in the *Daily Mail*, I could play in Siam, but not at Worcester in the county championship.

Thus, in the end, no one gained from the miserable saga. Gloucestershire lost an England batsman, who had given thirteen years' service; Worcestershire had to pay me a capped player's wages while I couldn't play in the championship – incidentally they did not represent any improvement for me – and Tom Pugh lasted two seasons. Despite having set a county record with a second-wicket partnership of 256 with him at Chesterfield, I knew he was not good enough to be consistent.

By a supreme irony Pugh was succeeded by my brother Ken. In view of the upset to the family caused by my departure, it was big of him to do so, and he rang me at Brisbane to ask if I would object. 'I've been asked to take over from Pugh because the side's in tatters,' he said. 'They want me to put a bit of discipline into it. Do you mind if I do it?' Of course I did not stand in his way. It's perhaps as well he didn't see my knowing smile. I wondered only at my brother's unswerving loyalty to Gloucestershire.

Later in life Ken became chairman, and in due course the skids were put under him, too, when his son David became captain in 1982. Officially the reason was to avoid any em-

barrassment over father and son occupying the two key positions in the club. Ken did not want to give up as Chairman.
Why should he? To me it was yet another example of cricket's
extraordinary facility for getting rid of its most valued ser-
vants.

In a different way it happened with England when Ray
Illingworth, who still had so much to offer, was given the
premature boot and his place was taken by Mike Denness.
Soon, in turn, Denness had the old heave-ho!

I think it would be fair to say there is a feeling of quiet
desperation in the mind of any cricketer summoned to
Lord's. Not that the hearing is conducted with anything but
scrupulous fairness, but the very air of unhurried judiciary,
and the fact that one's friends are intimately involved, is
rather unnerving. I did not leave with happy results on either
of my two appearances. The failure of Worcestershire's
application for immediate registration was disappointing, as
I felt I was the victim rather that the offender; but after the
second occasion, when I was found guilty of 'a serious breach
of discipline' and banned for three Tests, my feeling was one
of sickened despair.

It all started during the 1968 series with the Australians
when I was having a quiet drink in the Cricketers' Club in
London. Colin McDonald, the former Australian opening
batsman, introduced me to Tony Hunt of Vehicle and
General Insurance, a sports enthusiast and then chairman of
Luton Town Football Club. In the course of our conversation
I mentioned that Worcestershire had granted me a benefit for
1969. Without more ado he said, 'If you would like to come
and play at Luton one Sunday we will guarantee you four
figures from the club.'

Here, indeed, was an offer I could not refuse, for £1,000
was nearly a fifth of the benefit I had taken from Gloucestershire. At the time the fee for playing in a Test match was
£120.

So many promises made at a bar remain unfulfilled that I

took it with a pinch of salt, lest I be let down. Then there was
the problem of finding Sundays for benefit games, since the
John Player League began in 1969. The only date open to me
was in June during a Test with the West Indies at Old
Trafford. Obviously, I did not even know whether I would
be picked, but I took the precaution of seeking out Alec
Bedser, chairman of the selectors, and an old England colleague. Alec warned me that I could not play in both matches.
My answer was that, in this instance, Luton would have to
have priority as I had given an undertaking. Also I could not
afford to let the opportunity pass by. I had always given my
faithful best for England – Alec knew that – but with reluctance I told him to forget me for the Old Trafford Test. We
left it with Alec saying that he would contact Hunt, while I
reiterated my intention to appear at Luton unless he came up
with some other arrangement, whatever that might be. As far
as I was concerned the matter was in the hands of Bedser and
his selectors. When I learned of my selection for the Test, I
assumed everything had been taken care of and there could
be no official objection to my playing at Luton, where the
posters had long announced details of an exhibition match
between Tom Graveney's XI and Bobby Simpson's XI.

I have never been certain in my mind whether the selectors,
apart from the chairman, had a clear picture of my position
and my commitment to go to Luton on the rest day of the
Test. From subsequent conversations with two of the selectors, this would appear not to have been the case, but I was
left in no doubt on the evening of the first day of the Test
when Bedser told me I could not go to Luton. Dismayed I
asked 'How about my promise to them? What about the
money they promised me?' Bedser was more confident than
I was that Tony Hunt would still pay out even if I did not
turn up. And what of my obligation to the sponsors, who had
done an immense amount of work to make the occasion a
success, and the public of Luton?

Bedser reminded me that England always came first, as if
I needed reminding, and again said he would try and sort out

the problem. Unhappily he could not contact Hunt, who had entered hospital for a check-up, and nothing more was said until later that evening, the first day of the Test, when Bedser repeated his ban on the Luton match. In turn I told him that it was too late for me to pull out.

At the back of my mind I half hoped the organisers might be content for me to umpire, or just to make a token appearance, but the suggestion was never made. The actual performance, which was to cost me dearly, was an innings against some slow to very slow bowling by Richie Benaud and Bob Simpson. I couldn't have been injured if I'd tried! Moreover the state of the Test was so much in England's favour, with the West Indies following on – England won by ten wickets – that my major contribution was to all intents and purposes over. In what, alas, proved to be my last Test innings I was second top-scorer with 75 and I took part in a third-wicket stand of 128 with Geoff Boycott.

Some have since told me that my mistake was to be open about my intentions, and that had I just quietly left Manchester on the Saturday evening – and after all many of the team motored home and returned to the team's hotel on the Sunday evening – no one would have been the wiser, or cared too much even if it had come to light.

The next day was my forty-second birthday, and my 'present' was to learn over the loud-speakers while I was on the field that I had been reported to the disciplinary committee and would have to explain my action on the Thursday – the day the team for the next Test at Lord's was due to be chosen. I went to Lord's, and Gilbert Ashton, president of Worcestershire and representing the county, sat among a committee under Edmond King, of Warwickshire, and including Tom Pearce (Essex) and David Clark (Kent).

The major point to go against me was Bedser's assertion that he had told me of the position before the game, and not on the Thursday evening. The ruling was that I had been guilty of a 'serious breach of discipline'. I was severely reprimanded, and the selectors informed that I was not to be considered for the next three Test matches.

In the minutes it took to read the statement I knew it was goodbye England. Though Don Kenyon, a selector, a friend and my captain at Worcester, asked me before the final Test if I was still interested, I knew well enough not to take the enquiry to heart. In any case Yorkshire's Jackie Hampshire, who took my place, hit the first century by an Englishman on a Test début at Lord's. Yet by the time New Zealand, the visitors in the second half of the season, were at Lord's in late July, Hampshire was no longer in the side.

Edmond King's committee softened the pill by saying they had given full consideration to 'Graveney's long and out-standing contribution to English cricket and the various pressures on him in connexion with the match at Luton.'

Mr Hunt's impact on the sporting scene did not survive many years, and when the crash of Vehicle and General came it meant that Luton were obliged to sell their centre-forward to Newcastle United – a young fellow by the name of Malcolm Macdonald. Alec Stock, Luton's manager at the time, told him, 'Sorry, I don't want to lose you, but you'll have to go.' Macdonald, unabashed, hired a Rolls and travelled to Newcastle, and to lasting footballing fame, in style. My route led in the opposite direction. All the way to Brisbane, Australia.

4
A New Lease of Life

Though it would have taken much to convince me at the time
that it was all for the best, my break with Gloucestershire
proved to be a blessing in disguise and the pathway to a
highly satisfying second career. My mood had been of confused sadness rather than bitterness, but, in retrospect, I
think I needed a fresh environment and new challenges to
repair my broken pride and renew my zest for the game. I
owed plenty to Sir George Dowty for persuading me not to
abandon county cricket. 'Worcestershire are on the verge of
big things. You are just the man to tip the scales for us,' he
urged – honeyed words, which appealed to me, and, as events
proved, prophetic words.

My move to Worcester coincided with another fortunate
aspect of what I might call my rehabilitation period after the
depressions of the 'throwing' tour of Australia and the upset
with Gloucestershire. I had become a regular member of the
unofficial tours organised by the late Ron Roberts, who
passionately loved cricket and travel and was able to combine
both as a freelance journalist of distinction.

Moreover, he was something of a visionary with his 'mixed'
parties which brought together in the same dressing-room
cricketers who were often locked in contentious opposition.
Ron's imaginative concept of all players as a band of cricketing brothers engaged in playing with rather than against
each other made a mockery of politics and governments forever seeking to make use of sport for their own ends. All too

early in life Ron died, leaving the entire cricket world to mourn a cherished friend.

I had first gone with Ron to Johannesburg for three weeks in 1959 under Denis Compton's captaincy. His party included Godfrey Evans, Frank Tyson, Brian Close, the Australians Ian Craig, Bobby Simpson and leg-spinner Pete Philpott, and the brilliant New Zealander Bert Sutcliffe, who bravely returned to the land where he once took a fearful blow on the head from the fast bowler Neil Adcock. This was not, on the face of it, a significant occasion, but it had a special meaning for me as I set myself, as the Number 1 batsman from England and recently discarded by the selectors, the task of matching Sutcliffe and Simpson. As it was I made two crucial centuries and an 86, and felt I had not let myself down. Even to the most experienced player confidence is as necessary as applause to the actor. With it you feel fit to face the world; without it you feel unarmed.

I always remembered the words of Charlie Barnett: 'Your first duty is to your side, and when you have seen it into the right position your next duty is to yourself.' Some of the best players have been criticised as selfish – 'personal players' was the polite phrase – but it can be argued that, in looking after himself by stealing the bowling and so on, the star boosts his side. Extreme selfishness, however, is unacceptable. I tried to hide any inner feelings, and, on occasions, I have to admit I was far from the confident figure I might have presented. In my early days I would walk into the England dressing-room and look at the legendary figures around me – Len Hutton, Denis Compton, Peter May, Fred Trueman, Alec Bedser, Godfrey Evans, Trevor Bailey and so on – and wonder what I was doing there! It took some time to banish my complex that I was an intruder in such company.

Around the time my personal clouds were gathering over Bristol – I returned in time for my dismissal from the Gloucestershire captaincy – I was one of a twelve-strong party of internationals from England and Australia which toured Transvaal, Natal and Rhodesia. There were four Test

captains in the side: Ray Illingworth, Mike Smith, Richie
Benaud and Bobby Simpson – and when Richie was injured
in the first match, I took over. If serious criticisms were made
of my qualifications for the post they did not reach my ears
– a little fact I pass on to the county committee, who, by then,
had already long since decided to sack me!

I had an ideal opportunity to slip into serious competitive
gear in the months before my championship début for my new
county by taking part in the boldest of Ron Roberts' fertile
ideas – the first multi-racial world tour, on which we covered
40,000 miles, mostly by jet, and played in countries as far
apart as Rhodesia, Hong Kong, East Africa, India, Pakistan
and New Zealand. In all twenty-four players were recruited,
including nineteen of Test rank, among them the then captains of both England (Colin Cowdrey) and Australia (Richie
Benaud).

After a splendid performance against us for East Africa,
Ramanbhai Patel joined the party, which was under the joint
captaincy of Everton Weekes and Ray Lindwall for the first
part and Benaud for the second. Apart from the English,
Australians and West Indians there were, at different stages,
South Africans, the Rhodesian Colin Bland, the Pakistanis –
Hanif Mohammad and Saeed Ahmed – and the outstanding
Indian leg-spinner Subhas Gupte. The South African contingent included Basil D'Oliveira, and it was this first meeting
of ours, I like to think, that persuaded him eventually to try
his luck at county level and, in particular, to join Worcestershire.

I knew and Basil knew that promise and fulfilment are
uneasy companions in cricket but nobody knew better than
I at the time the value of having a voice saying, 'You're good.
You can do it.' Here was I, straining every nerve, as the joint
senior English player with Colin Cowdrey, to reassure myself
that I was at least as good as the best of the overseas batsmen
in the party. (With all modesty I record that my confidence

was boosted by two centuries and three other scores in the nineties.)

Everton Weekes, like myself, was one of six players to complete the whole of that fabulous trip with Ron Roberts, and it was the first time black players from the West Indies were received in Southern Africa (as distinct from South Africa, for the side did not go south of Saiisbury on the continent), and they happily played alongside Roy McLean and Neil Adcock. McLean and Weekes became particularly close friends, but Adcock and McLean were not allowed entry to India and Pakistan. Bland, however, came into the side in an emergency at Dacca, now the capital of Bangladesh, but then in the east wing of Pakistan.

The players of so many races mixed harmoniously and public relations were good, but there were two souring incidents to serve as painful reminders of racial prejudices. In the first half of the tour the selectors were Ray Lindwall, Everton Weekes, Ron Roberts, the manager, and myself in the role of senior pro. We stopped for a pre-arranged meal at Gwelo on the way from Bulawayo to an up-country centre, and I led the way to the bar for a drink to ease our dust-filled throats. 'Four gin and tonics, please,' I said to a hard-looking woman serving behind the bar. As the drinks were being poured Everton, the last of the company, walked in. The barmaid looked up and said, 'Your bar's round the corner. You're not allowed in here. Get out.'

After a few emphatic words from me to tell her what she could do with her gin and tonic, we left in disgust. I don't think Everton, who I am pleased to call a friend, ever forgave anyone in Southern Africa for his humiliation – and who could blame him? It was as if a menacing shadow had passed over us, and I felt sickened for I knew Everton to be a very fine human being as well as a great cricketer.

Sonny Ramadhin, an orphan raised in a Canadian Mission School in Trinidad and a unique spin bowler, also felt the chill wind of racialism in another hotel in Rhodesia. He was ordered out of a barber's shop by a youth who could have done with a wash and haircut himself. Understandably Sonny, the mildest of little men, was so incensed that he wanted to pack up there and then and return home. He said he was so disgusted that he didn't want to know Rhodesia any more, and it needed the combined persuasion of manager, captains and team-mates to talk him into staying with the party. Fortunately he did, and completed the entire tour, but it was touch and go.

It scarcely needs saying that there was no hint of discord between the players – black, white, brown or any shade in between. Hanif Mohammad, Pakistan's 'Little Master', did display one idiosyncrasy which was new to me among crick-eters. At Salisbury he insisted on having his lunch at the team's hotel instead of at the ground, where the food did not appeal to him. The rest of us enjoyed the joke.

In October 1963 Alf Gover took a Commonwealth side to Pakistan, captained by Peter Richardson and consisting mainly of English and West Indian players. The only non-first-class player was Basil D'Oliveira.

Basil, a Cape Coloured, had been plucked from obscurity by the agency of John Arlott to Middleton in the Central Lancashire League, who, at the time of the tour, wanted him to sign a new two-year contract. He had to make up his mind whether to stay in the League or extend his ambitions. We were having a drink at the Hotel Metropole, Karachi, and discussing his problem, when he said, 'I'm getting cold feet. I don't think I'm good enough for county cricket.' Having seen him play a marvellous knock at Nairobi and score an impressive 57 at Nkana, I told him bluntly not to talk rubbish. I also laid it on a bit thick by adding, 'You will go into it and you will be as great a success as anybody who has ever played the game.'

When I told Basil he was already better than a lot of first-class players, he was sold on county cricket, and, by a supreme irony, he had to make a choice between Worcestershire and Gloucestershire. Curiously Lancashire, the county Basil would have joined like a shot, had no interest in him, as they had just taken on Sonny Ramadhin, and Cyril Washbrook had apparently dismissed him as a 'Saturday afternoon slogger'. Obviously I wanted to see his talents at Worcester and I pressed home the self-evident truth that it was in his best interests to go to a strong team. After all, one good turn deserved another.

Strange that in years to come our careers should be identified with England and Worcestershire, we should be in the same Rest of the World XI to celebrate the independence of Barbados, and – stranger still – that I should play an unwitting part in Dolly's selection for a Test match which led to cricket's biggest crisis since bodyline.

In 1968 Basil had lost his place after the first Test against Australia – despite 87 not out in the second innings – and was having an ordinary time with Worcestershire. Before the last Test at the Oval Roger Prideaux dropped out with tonsilitis, and I had a phone call from England's captain, Colin Cowdrey.

'Prideaux isn't well and we are struggling for a batsman. How's Basil shaping?' he asked.

As Basil had just scored a century and was running back to form, I took up his cause. 'He's looking in great nick,' I enthused. 'He's coming right back to what he was.'

Cowdrey listened and rang off saying, 'That's good news. I think we might pick him.'

Basil made 158, John Edrich 164 and I supported with 63, and D'Oliveira also secured a vital wicket. Oddly he was not in the original party for South Africa that winter, and I was with him when he heard the shattering news on the radio. Subsequently he replaced the injured Tom Cartwright, and South Africa, wrongly charging England with duplicity, called the tour off.

My visits to South Africa were really fun tours, free from the fierce competition and nationalism engendered by official Tests. Therefore we were mainly insulated from the controversies of apartheid. Nevertheless I was sorry to miss the two

MCC tours I might have made to South Africa, first in 1956 and then in 1965, in which year Mike Brearley was preferred. By then I was only on the fringe of Test cricket, but my omission from Peter May's side in 1956 puzzles me to this day, especially as Cyril Washbrook and the Rev. David Sheppard, who played in the final Test of the home series, were not available, and I topped the national averages with 2,397 runs.

A persistent dressing-room rumour was that I paid the penalty for having cried off with an injury to my right hand for the fourth Test against Ian Johnson's 1956 Australians at Old Trafford, and even that I was guilty of a dubious enterprise to ensure my selection for the winter tour. The rumour did me little credit, and I cannot believe anyone knowing me would give credence to the theory. The facts are quite simple. After three failures in four innings in the first two Tests, I was dropped. Fair enough; no complaints.

England had lost the second Test and 'Gubby' Allen and his selectors had to look for quick remedies, one of which was to recall Cyril Washbrook, himself a selector, for the crucial third Test at Headingley. Gubby's inspired insistence that England needed Washbrook's experience in the middle order was justified to the hilt when Cyril, who had last played in the 1950–51 series, helped Peter May halt a collapse with a score of 98, and so played a major part in Australia's defeat.

After that I was surprised to be called up again for the fourth Test at Old Trafford – the Test in which Jim Laker made history with nineteen wickets. I was looking forward to re-establishing myself, but unhappily I was hit on the back of my right hand by Brian Statham at Blackpool and I knew my chances of being fit were remote. On the Wednesday, the day before the Test, I saw a specialist at Manchester. He told me I had no chance and gave me a written report which I duly passed on to the chairman. I did not go to the customary net practice for the simple reason that I knew it would be a pointless formality to have a fitness test. Possibly that was an error of judgment, but nothing altered the basic fact that I could not hold a bat properly, nor stand the jarring of ball on bat without pain.

Presumably, had I attended the nets and gone through the rigmarole of a test in front of the selectors, Press and so forth, the final decision would have still been passed to me – and that would have been a 'sorry, can't do it' verdict. One vital factor was that I knew I could not have fielded normally, and, as it was, my replacement Alan Oakman, a specialist close-in fielder, took five catches as Jim Laker pressed home his advantage, as only Jim could, on a turning pitch. Oakman did a job I knew I could not have done on that particular occasion.

I stayed to watch the first day's play, and before regretfully leaving I shook hands all round and wished the boys luck. Since then I have been told more times than I care to remember and by more people than I care to count that I must have made a tactical mistake by using my injured hand to shake hands. As if that proved a thing! I still find it preposterous and inconceivable that such a bizarre legend should be attached to me, or, indeed, to any player of unquestioned loyalty, as I think I proved to be over seventy-nine Tests and many tours.

When I was a guest at Gubby Allen's eightieth birthday celebration at Lord's I was fleetingly tempted to ask what the reason was for his selectors' casting me aside for the Oval Test and the subsequent tour – merely to satisfy my curiosity, as I was the in-form batsman of the season. To quote from *Wisden*: 'Graveney was outstanding. He kept his place at the head of the county [Gloucestershire] aggregates and averages, increased his championship total by over five hundred and, above all, batted in a confident and attractive style which made him a favourite with the crowds. Often, in unhelpful conditions, he stood alone, scoring masterfully while most of his colleagues failed. Few of those present at the game against Glamorgan at Newport in August will forget how he dominated play so completely that he scored 200, including three 6's and twenty-four 4's, out of a total of 298.'

It cannot have happened many times, if at all, for the

batsman heading the national averages in a difficult season
for batsmen, to miss out on an immediate major overseas
tour, even when one of the batting places was booked by a
returning hero of the magnetic appeal of Denis Compton.
Like everyone I rejoiced to see him back for England after
his serious knee operation and celebrating with a typical 94.
Gubby Allen right again! Rightly Denis went to South Africa,
but if I might make one observation, it is that neither of the
two preferred to me for those tours – Alan Oakman in 1956
and Mike Brearley in 1965 – succeeded in winning a Test
place on tours of the Republic.

Selectors, bless 'em, have their passing whims and fancies,
like all of us, and there will never be an occasion when players,
Press and the public will agree one hundred per cent on the
choice of a Test team or a touring party. The chosen captain
has to have his important say, and his ideas might not neces-
sarily agree with those of the other selectors. Captains are apt
to resist trying out youngsters, for they know they are likely
to carry the can for misadventures with a badly balanced side.
How, for instance, did England come to send three off-spinners to Australia in 1982–83? Also, with today's large fees
and incentives at stake, a captain has more reason to insist on
what he regards as his best side – no kids, no experiments.

In these days, partly because the number of Test-class
players had declined, it is difficult to comprehend the situation in 1962, when England made no fewer than six changes
(and I quote from *Wisden*) 'to give some players a chance and
avoid calling too heavily on counties engaged in the fight for
the championship'. In came Colin Cowdrey, Ken Barrington,
David Allen, Ray Illingworth, Len Coldwell and David
Larter; out went Tony Lock, Fred Trueman, Brian Statham,
Fred Titmus, Geoff Pullar and myself. Yet England still beat
Pakistan by ten wickets.

Test selection, and the general management of cricket,
in an age of stern competition from television and an ever-
expanding range of other sports, is becoming so complex and

professionalised that I think it unwise to debar old players merely because they go into television, broadcasting and journalism. To me it seems an enormous wastage of talent and experience that the likes of Trevor Bailey, Fred Trueman and Ted Dexter are not eligible for the selection committee. They know the game inside out, are *au fait* with current form, and fill every requirement for the job. It is absurd to imagine they would blurt out committee secrets in print or on the air.

If cricket is to survive without gimmicks and a lowering of standards, it is imperative that the best available talent should always be on tap, and it seems folly to rule out those who are with the media.

In recent years it has been seriously put to me at least twice that I should become a selector. Nothing would please me more and, what is more important, I am sure I could make a useful contribution, particularly with my extensive knowledge of overseas conditions. I would be prepared to give my time and effort, but for cricket also to expect me to surrender part of my livelihood is asking too much.

5
Heady Years with the Champions

As one who had two counties, it might appear impertinent of me to declare that soccer-style transfers are not for cricket. In principle moves without just cause are wrong, but I contend that mine was a just cause – otherwise I would have left the game. One noted cricket writer at the time warned of the dangers of a player 'taking a £5,400 benefit and then selling himself, theoretically at any rate, to the highest bidder'.

Having faced a drop of £250 a year in pay – fortunately Worcestershire made it up right away – I thought it a singularly fatuous observation, but, oddly, it might have some credence in these times when it has been shown that a coach and horses can be ridden through cricket's regulations by invoking laws relating to restraint of trade.

I suppose, as Barry Wood proved when he left Lancashire for Derbyshire after taking a £62,429 benefit, I could in this age have taken my lawyer with me to Lord's and been allowed to play in the championship for my adopted county without delay. Wood, whose dispute was over pay, had his ban reduced from three months to a nominal one month. I had to qualify for a season, and after all the hassle and publicity over my case I was vastly amused that my invitation from Lord's to play in the first Test against Pakistan the next year was addressed to Gloucestershire County Cricket Club!

*　　*　　*

When you get a little older you have to have something to aim at.

While it was frustrating to have to sit on the sidelines watching first-class cricket, the summer of 1961 was not entirely wasted. From a professional viewpoint the worst feature was that it put me out of the Test orbit, and, of course, out of the limelight. On the other hand it enabled me to take stock of myself. That much was expected of me was evident from the rapturous reception I received on going out to bat in the Australian tourists' opening fixture in which, as it was a non-championship game, I was allowed to play. I was certainly on my mettle. Critics often accused me of being a somewhat casual batsman and over-relaxed, but you are what you are. Players like David Gower and John Murray are often accused of being too casual – but it only happens when they lose their wicket! I never thought I lacked concentration at the wicket, and I think that my record of over 47,000 runs proves my point.

Another and more human reason why I wanted to do well for Worcestershire was as a rebuke to Gloucestershire – just to show 'em! My first ball for my new county was a long hop from Richie Benaud, which was either due to cold fingers or compassion, but I missed it. Fortunately I buckled down to make 36, the second top score. I also took 152 not out off Cambridge University, the only time in my career I had the good fortune to play at Fenner's. There was a two-day fixture for MCC against the Club Cricket Conference, whose fast bowler, a certain John Price from Wembley, made me work extremely hard for my 100 runs. Price was very impressive, and it was not long before he went to Middlesex and bowled for England. My runs invited the memorable snide letter which said, 'Lovely to see you smashing the club cricket bowlers all over Lord's when it doesn't matter. Why can't you do it when it does matter?' Friends in cricket come and go.

The Second XI championship was another new experience. We had Duncan Fearnley, now a well-known cricket bat manufacturer, to score over a thousand runs; youngsters like Alan Ormrod and Duggie Slade; while Fred Rumsey, soon to bowl for England under Somerset's colours, headed our bowling averages. I remember meeting the young Scot, Mike Denness, then qualifying for Kent, who also had David Constant, the umpire-to-be, Colin Page and fast bowler Fred Ridgeway, my old touring companion in India and Pakistan. Another famous umpire-to-be was Dickie Bird at Leicester, which county had a young fast bowler, Peter Broughton, who was being tipped as another Frank Tyson. Broughton took 95 wickets for Leicestershire II that summer, but unfortunately he did not come through. Yorkshire II's batting was headed by Chris Balderstone and Geoff Boycott.

I also had five outings and two centuries for Dudley, which did not prevent them from finishing bottom of the Birmingham League! I used to be secretly amused, having played in 48 Tests for England, to see my name as the pro at the bottom of the team-sheet – Graveney T.W. It reminded me that once Freddie Titmus was on the balcony of the Middlesex dressing-room before a match at Lord's when he heard a loud-speaker team announcement: 'For F.J. Titmus read Titmus F.J.'

To be frank I was not over-impressed by the organisation at Dudley at the time. Alan Ormrod also had a few games and they didn't think he could play at all! Much the same, I was later told, was said of Ron Headley and Norman Gifford, both future Test men.

It is a curious fact that sometimes club cricketers have low opinions of professionals who have played in the same side, but the classic instance must be the ready dismissal of Ian Botham after his season in Melbourne grade cricket as a young player. While it is true that on paper his performances were no great shakes, I was surprised to hear former Australian Test men at the Melbourne Centenary match say that Botham wouldn't make some of their grade sides. Mind you much the same thing has been said of established internationals touring Australia, but in Botham's case I think enlightenment has dawned since 1981.

One of my bitter disappointments during my qualifying year was to be discarded by the Scarborough Festival. I had been a regular for many seasons, and I had looked forward to the prospect of at least finishing the period on top notch with some first-class innings. I was not sure whether it was merely a question of 'out of sight, out of mind', but I must admit that I was upset to be ignored without even being offered an explanation, and when I was invited the following year I declined with a suitable reply.

In the last three weeks of July I went to Bermuda with Stuart Surridge – a compensation for missing the Scarborough Festival. As I had been to the delectable island before, with Hutton's team in 1953 on the way to the West Indies (the calm before the storm!), I was forearmed and able to cope with the extra bounce and turn of the matting-over-concrete wickets. The grounds, as enchanting as the island itself, are tiny, and I remember Peter May hitting the ball so hard against a miniature cliff face on one side of the boundary that it rebounded to the wicket. The umpire would not be convinced that the ball had come back off the wall and allowed only one run!

Another event of that visit was a four-ball golf match between Denis Compton and Charlie Palmer and two local opponents, who drank five gins and tonics before lunch, beer, gin and tonic during the meal and Van der Hum liqueur afterwards. Play then started with a gin and tonic being brought to the second tee. Palmer and Compton took the opportunity to toss theirs away while their opponents were addressing the ball. At the third hole the home pair opened a bottle of Van der Hum, which they had drunk by the ninth, whereupon they retired to the club-house for three more gins and tonic.

At the tenth the caddy produced another gin and tonic, and at the eleventh a bottle of brandy, which was empty by the sixteenth, at which stage the home pair conceded a blurry defeat, oblivious to the fact that Palmer and Compton had left a trail of gin, liqueur, beer and brandy in the rough behind bushes and in bunkers! The course must have been almost awash.

Bermuda had two sharp bowlers, and a left-arm thrower, who turned and bounced at medium pace, an awkward customer, but my enjoyment was enhanced by a 205 not out and 104 in the representative matches and, dare I mention it, a bowling analysis of 7 for 34. To an outsider it would be easy to dismiss such performances as of no consequence, but the longer I played the tantalising game of cricket the more I realised the value of attitudes and inner confidence. As many batsmen are defeated by the wrong approach and anxieties as by bowlers, and Bermuda was all part of the relaunching of my first-class career. In my first Second XI match on my return I broke a finger to end my season!

By the time I was qualified for Worcestershire I felt ready to meet any challenge. I had held my own with the best in the world on Ron Roberts' tours, and Worcestershire without my help had climbed to fourth place. Whether my first season with my new county would have been such a success if a straightforward slip catch had been held when I was ten in the second innings in the opening match with Pakistan is a matter of conjecture. The chance should have been swallowed, but it went down, and I went on to make 117 – not one of my best centuries by a long way, yet one of the most important. When I was out after five hours, skipper Don Kenyon was waiting at the top of the pavilion steps to present me with my Worcestershire cap.

A feeling of sublime relief engulfed me, for it had been the strangest of emotions walking to the wicket in new colours with so much expected of me. Normally I was not unduly nervous, but that was one of the three occasions when I was surprised at my own tension. The others were in my 1966 come-back at Lord's against the West Indies, and two years later at Old Trafford, probably due to the fact that I had never really done well against Australia. I must have been a borderline selection until I scored 96 and 39 not out in the third Test at Edgbaston – an auspicious match for me as I took over the captaincy from the injured Colin Cowdrey.

Making a big score so early in the season was another happy augury for my new career at Worcester. The older player, while usually comforted by the knowledge that he has done it all the year before, likes to get a 50 or a 100 as soon as he can, if only to nourish his self-assurance and allay any nagging doubts creeping in his mind. Believe me, that hard-fought century off Pakistan on a dodgy pitch was as sweet as any I scored at county level.

From then on it was roses all the way: five championship centuries, and sharing a third-wicket county record of 314 against Somerset with Martin Horton, who made 233 at a speed which left me gasping; and two more centuries for England. I was second in the national averages, fractionally below Reg Simpson, who completed only twenty innings, and second to Peter Parfitt for England. Parfitt averaged 113.33 and I had 100.25 – a figure I would settle for any time.

What was even better was Worcestershire's triumph as runners-up, the prelude to the halcyon seasons as champions in 1964 and 1965. I am sure the stimulus of playing in a successful side helped me enormously, and I suppose my attitude changed accordingly.

Every match meant something, the public were as one behind the team – how invigorating it was to arrive on a Monday morning to see the ground filling up and hear an expectant buzz of conversation – and after a couple of years that excellent England and Worcestershire bowler Len Coldwell probably hit the nail on the head when he said to me: 'You used to *play* for Gloucestershire, but you *work* for Worcestershire.'

Local support from one of the smallest county populations in the first-class game was so faithful that any offering by a player less than his best would have been an act of base treachery. For three years or so, despite an unaccountable team slump in 1963, I had a feeling at the back of my mind that I was the best batsman in England, or at least comparable with the best, though I wasn't playing for England. It was a belief in myself which stood me in good stead when I did return to the Test side in 1966, though paradoxically I don't think I was as good then as I had been in the previous three years, because of age as much as anything.

Worcester's wickets, prepared to achieve a result, helped bowlers and taxed both the technical skills and the concentration of batsmen – some of the county teams did not even like coming to the ground – but those casting stones at us in the first championship year of 1964 had to counter the fact that Worcestershire achieved eleven victories away to seven at home. Worcestershire had match-winning bowlers in Len Coldwell and Jack Flavell; splendid supports in Bob Carter and Jim Standen, the footballer and outstanding fielder; fine spinners in Norman Gifford and Martin Horton; and there could not have been a better captain than Don Kenyon. When I succeeded him I knew I had something to live up to.

Kenyon was unlucky not to take the championship in 1962. We finished our programme before Yorkshire, who had to defeat Glamorgan in their last fixture at Harrogate to take the title. When our last game finished, the crowd massed in front of the pavilion in premature celebration. Kenyon led the players on to the balcony, champagne corks popped in the dressing-room, and we dispersed to spend three days in purgatory.

When the news arrived of a wash-out on the second day at Harrogate it looked long odds on Worcestershire's title, but all hands went to the pumps, so to speak, from the early hours to ensure play on the final day and, before a huge crowd, Yorkshire's spinners Don Wilson and Ray Illingworth brought victory with two hours to spare, and the championship by a margin of four points, or 0.13 on average.

Years later Tony Lewis, later Glamorgan's captain, told me Glamorgan buckled under the sheer Yorkshire-ism of the crowd. One critic wrote that, if he were a captain aiming to win a crucial match, the opposition he would choose would be Glamorgan. Yet Glamorgan did not have to wait long to be champions themselves! A strange game, cricket.

Worcestershire had also to sweat it out when the title eventually did come to them in 1964, after sixty-five years – most of which time was spent nearer the other end of the table – and a few months before the club's centenary. The reader might be interested to know that the clincher was at home to Gloucestershire, who were defeated by an innings after Worcestershire had declared at 398 for 3 – Don Kenyon 114, Ron Headley 103 not out and Graveney 57 – with two hours to spare.

Warwickshire, still in the chase, needed to win at Southampton and, while the players gathered in the committee room to listen to the frequent radio bulletins, over a thousand spectators gathered in front of the pavilion. The tension mounted as Warwickshire, set to score 314 at 90 an hour by Colin Ingleby-Mackenzie's declaration, went boldly for victory. They finished 17 short. Moments passed before Don Kenyon, seemingly a hardened old pro, could bring himself to speak. Worcestershire went on to win the last two matches with a flourish and had a 41-point margin in the end, the highest margin since Surrey's amazing 94 points in 1957. Such was the excitement among the crowd on that memorable evening at Worcester that, had Ingleby-Mackenzie's declaration led to a Warwickshire victory, half the city would probably have set out in search of the Hampshire captain! In point of fact it was a fair and astute declaration, and brought him a splendid victory.

In common with all the players, I had a lot of time for the ex-submariner Colin, whose carefree spirit tended often to camouflage his tactical awareness. He was a calculating gambler, and teams liked to play against Hampshire because a game would find expression and not be stifled by oppressive caution. Worcestershire certainly had cause to appreciate Colin's attitude a year later when the championship was retained, this time by only four points on the strength of ten victories in the final eleven matches. Worcestershire only went to the top five minutes before close of play in the last match at Hove. But as Basil D'Oliveira rightly said, 'That's the only time it counts.'

Hampshire were the only team to stop us in our final charge, and that when the ninth pair, Peter Sainsbury and David ('Butch') White, hung on for a draw at Worcester. There were fifteen lbw decisions in a remarkable match, including myself twice to Derek Shackleton, a bowler of extraordinary skills and accuracy. He would never give an inch. I regard the 80 I made in the first innings as one of my best innings ever.

When we went to Bournemouth in late August to play them again, we had to win to hold off Northamptonshire, who could not have been pleased with three declarations, including one by Colin Ingleby-Mackenzie when Hampshire were still 146 behind with four wickets to go at lunch on the third day. At the time it was forbidden to concede an innings, so Worcestershire declared at 0 for 0 after one ball bowled by Ingleby-Mackenzie. Unfortunately for Colin, a strong sun suddenly emerged from behind the clouds and the pitch was transformed from a slow pudding into an impossible batting surface. Hampshire were dismissed for 31 by Jack Flavell and Len Coldwell in 16.3 overs and sixty-five minutes. Not a single batsman reached double figures. It all showed that even the strongest sides need luck.

As late as 23 July, we were ninth in the table with only three victories to our credit, and I have often been asked to explain Worcestershire's Jekyll and Hyde performance. Really there was no logical reason, for we were as strong in batting and bowling, and equally well led, in the first part, when nothing went right, as we were at the end when everything went right.

A perk for taking the title was to take the championship pennant some 34,000 miles into seven different countries, some of whom had never seen an English county before. For myself, I never expected to score centuries at Singapore, Salisbury, Kowloon, Hong Kong and Ballygunge! We saw

Nairobi, Bangkok, Que Que and Honolulu. Little wonder the players said, 'Become a cricketer and see the world.'

To my regret Worcestershire did not come close to a championship in my three years as Don Kenyon's successor. To be realistic it was never on, as the old side had largely broken up – four of the last championship side had gone by 1968, including Kenyon and Flavell – and the county was at a transitional stage. Nevertheless Worcestershire were seventh in my first year – when I was away for half the county programme on Test call; dropped to twelfth when Len Coldwell left and the overseas pair of Glenn Turner and Vanburn Holder were on tour in England, and rose to sixth in 1970, when *Wisden* published a photograph of me leaving the field for the last time and described me as a 'batting institution'.

I always wished I had been able to take a century off Gloucestershire, though it was not as if I did not do well against them. My best was an undefeated 87, and in my benefit game I was 59 when I had to retire hurt. Being out of the Test side at least enabled me to concentrate on Worcestershire. Curiously I had not set my heart on scoring a hundred centuries, but when my hundredth came against Northamptonshire I was, in one sense, a little surprised; in another, highly delighted.

It was simple to slip into a routine. For home matches I would drive the children to school, aiming to arrive by 9.30 to have at least fifteen minutes' serious batting in the nets, with Jack Flavell occasionally using a new ball against me. I always firmly believed there was only one way to use nets, and that was for both batsman and bowler to put in as much effort and concentration as if they were in the middle. I sometimes looked askance at the casualness of England on tour in the old days before there was a manager to take special responsibility for practice. Some merely went through the motions, which was a waste of time. I also placed a lot of importance on catching practice – I held 547 catches in my career, mainly at slip – and the last half-hour before play was spent in relaxation.

Away from home I went for an early breakfast and a gentle loosener, usually a stroll around the town. The modern fetish for exercises and gymnastic exercises fascinates rather than convinces me. If I had been obliged to follow the now accepted routine, I am sure I would not have been prepared for cricket, either physically or mentally, and for all the attention to fitness the injury-rate is far higher now than it was before it all began. Bowlers like Alec Bedser, Freddie Trueman and Brian Statham had a workload far beyond that of their modern counterparts. The same can be said of the number of innings played by batsmen of my generation compared with the current one.

At their peak Len Coldwell and Jack Flavell were very fine bowlers. When I first saw Flavell he was a real tearaway, very quick, but the ball went anywhere. When, however, he shortened his run to around twelve to fourteen paces, he got in so close to the stumps that he was always hitting them with his bowling hand in his delivery strides. From first slip I could see the seam of the ball coming down the pitch absolutely upright and never rotating, and at the end of an over I would pick it up and notice that the only marks were on the stitches of the seam. On either side the ball was virgin smooth, as if it had never been used. Not only was it 'seam up' bowling, but Jack's line was middle stump to middle stump, with his front foot going right across to the spot on middle and leg or middle where the batsman made his mark. The ball went as straight as it was possible to go, and, as Jack didn't know which way the ball would divert after hitting the seam, the batsman certainly couldn't know either. It also meant there was the minimum of time for the slip catchers to adjust if a chance came their way.

I remember a critic being rather scathing of Norman O'Neill being repeatedly hit on the inside of the knee in a Test at Old Trafford against Flavell. 'O'Neill was incapable of defending himself,' it was written, but I sympathised because I understood only too well the batsman's problems. Jack had the competition of many class fast bowlers in his prime, otherwise he would assuredly have played for England more than four times.

It was on another Commonwealth tour to Pakistan, this time under the managership of Alf ('The Colonel') Gover, that I struck up a friendship with Billy Ibadulla which was to bring Glenn Turner to Worcestershire. Over half a million watched the six matches. In the second representative match at Lahore I scored 164 in the first innings and 107 in the second, when Billy also made 103 not out. Billy, a Pakistani who had qualified for Warwickshire – the hard way for three years, as he had played in a match in his homeland which had been largely rained off! – spotted Turner on a visit to Otago Boys' High School while on a coaching tour.

Ibadulla, convinced that Turner had great potential, re-commended him to Warwickshire, and he earned enough as a baker on night shifts to journey to England. Unfortunately, on arrival Turner, then 19, found that Warwickshire had their full quota of overseas players. Cynics used to say that Warwickshire had one or two *Warwickshire* players. Ibadulla rang me and asked if Turner could come for a trial at Worces-ter. I took one look at this frail youngster and recognised a very special talent, and I told Worcestershire to grab him before another county showed an interest. He was so correct in technique and organisation that he had all the hallmarks of a superb batsman in the making. I went on public record as saying that he would be one of the leading batsmen in the world in the seventies, but at the start he had to change his attitude which, with no disrespect, was the same as Geoff Boycott's – that occupation of the crease was the basis of batting success. In his first year or so Glenn Turner betrayed his high ability with a painful slowness. Fifties in three hours were all too often his ration, until, miraculously, he dis-covered his true cricketing identity in the John Player's County League – that was its title in its inauguration season of 1969.

A year later at Chelmsford Essex made 234 for 7 in their forty overs, thanks to an innings of 95 by their captain, the

swashbuckling Brian ('Tonker') Taylor, in an opening stand
of 122. Worcestershire had to score six an over and my
thoughts can well be imagined when, after seven overs, only
seven runs had been scored – all by Ron Headley – and only
twelve from eight overs. I was pacing up and down the
balcony, making urgent signs for them to get on with it, when
Essex brought on their spinners, Ray East and Robin Hobbs.
Suddenly shots began to flow in every direction, and in eleven
overs 70 runs were scored. Turner hit the ball over the top
with such effect that he raced to 60, and, though Essex won
by eleven runs, he became a different batsman from then on.
In twenty-four championship matches he scored 2,346 runs,
set up a new county record of ten centuries, and was involved
in thirteen out of twenty-one stands of a century or more.

Apart from a slight hiccup mid-way through the seventies
against the really quick bowlers, Turner was one of two
batsmen I would pick out from the whole decade. The other
was Viv Richards. They were the two best without a doubt.

The longer Glenn played limited-over cricket – which
became too much for me – the more devastating he became,
and if the mood took him he was almost impossible to contain.
He picked up the ball on length. If it was a certain length it
was to go in a certain direction, and he had a whip shot with
his bottom hand which sent the ball scorching through mid-
wicket off a delivery just short of a length and, incredibly,
almost with a straight bat.

Another overseas player to come through to Test status at
Worcester was the hugely likeable West Indian bowler Vanburn Holder. When he arrived from Barbados he delivered
the ball from the far edge of the crease, which often meant it
strayed down the leg-side, and so reduced his chances of
getting lbw decisions – though I have noticed the style is no
serious handicap to Jeff Thomson in Australia! 'Vanny' had
a receptive ear to advice, got closer to the stumps and became
a very useful bowler indeed.

I am sure that playing for Worcestershire made both Turner and Holder into internationals, a situation which brought

a conflict between my loyalty to England and my loyalty to Worcestershire, not to mention my affection for the two players. The fact was that, until the counties saw sense at last and put restrictions on the numbers of overseas players – albeit by a lengthy and tortuous process – English cricket was nothing more than a university for the players of other countries. By all means allow one established star per county of the class of Sir Gary Sobers, Barry Richards, Mike Procter or Clive Lloyd, but it was nothing short of preposterous folly to help develop international teams, notably the West Indies, Pakistan and New Zealand, at England's expense.

While England's strengths were eroded, particularly in key positions, other countries grew increasingly powerful. Prime examples of this effect were Viv Richards and Glenn Turner. Clearly both belonged to an élite class, but had they not played in county cricket I am convinced it would have taken them a lot longer to reach maturity. How ironical the situation when England became virtually the home ground of so many teams 'visiting' England! Once England had an advantage when playing at home, as some overseas sides found the conditions difficult – English players have equal problems in acclimatising abroad – but it largely disappeared. There was a fascination in seeing how well the touring teams adapted to English conditions.

Swing and seam bowling no longer held any terrors for the opposition, for the simple reason that the majority of the West Indians and Pakistanis encountered it daily in the championship or the cup competitions. The Richardses, the Lloyds and, going back a little, the Kanhais, had seen it all before. They were as used to it as the home team. What's more, I am sure the large numbers of overseas players have diminished the appeal of Test matches. At one time the overseas greats were names to be seen only occasionally. Now they can be seen at any time, and, if familiarity has not bred contempt, it has stripped international cricket of part of its glamour – its curiosity value if you like.

One does not have to go back all that many years to recall

the excitement of the arrival of the Australians or the West Indies – in the dressing-rooms there was a real thrill of expectation – but now there are so many tours, and the players are so well known, that one series follows another almost as a matter of routine. There can be no question that there are far too many Tests, often of the most dubious standard, and the regulars are clocking up appearances which alter all values.

6
To Queensland on the Rebound

My suspension after the lamentable Luton affair in 1969 left me shedding a few inward tears and with that feeling of empty regret which always follows a wholly avoidable episode. I remain convinced that I was a victim, not an offender.

In practical terms the decision of the disciplinary sub-committee of the Test and County Cricket Board spelt the end of the road for me after seventy-nine Tests. Surely only those with hearts of stone would deny that it was an emotional wrench for me. After the peaks and troughs of Test cricket both at home and abroad, the final curtain had come down on my international career in a committee room at Lord's. Wryly I accepted that the sentimental farewell, perhaps before an appreciative crowd, who understood that I had always given of my best for England, followed by 'champers' in the dressing-room, was not for me.

I felt wounded, but determined not to harbour a grievance. My mood left me open to offers, and, strangely, a tentative overture had been made to me during that last fatal Test at Old Trafford. During the match I had renewed acquaintance with Clem Jones, the Lord Mayor of Brisbane, a notable character in Queensland and with a reputation for getting things done. Over a drink in the committee room he told me he was on the look-out for a coach for Queensland. Could I make a recommendation?

Half-jokingly I replied, 'You had better wait until after

Sunday and my benefit match at Luton. I might do the job myself.' At that stage of the dispute, however, it had not occurred to me that it would end with a three-match suspension from Test cricket. Far less was there any plan to migrate to Australia.

Clearly, however, the seed for taking on Graveney as coach had been implanted in Jones' mind, and the pain of my punishment was softened by the swift follow-up of an invitation to Jackie and myself to travel to Queensland on a fact-finding mission. We travelled to the 'Sunshine State', breaking the journey at Fiji, in style. No royal couple could have been better treated.

I was also registered by Queensland as a player for the Sheffield Shield and cup competitions, but my experience was painfully terminated in my second game against Victoria at Brisbane on one of the worst pitches it was my misfortune to encounter. After three days of rain the pitch had not been rolled, and 'Froggy' Thomson, a fast but erratic bowler who was soon to play against Ray Illingworth's side, twice hit me on the same spot on my left arm. The second blow caused a fracture, and the score-sheet for the match read:

	First Innings	Second Innings
T. W. Graveney	retired hurt o	absent hurt o

Too late I decided it had been a mistake to get in line with the ball on a pitch where the ball was spitting like a cobra off a length. My admiration for the old masters of the class of Sir Jack Hobbs, Wally Hammond and Herbert Sutcliffe, who not only survived but scored runs on the old-fashioned Australian stickies, became boundless.

Rather than deterring me, however, the accident helped to clear my mind, and when Jackie and I returned home, we decided to invest our future in Australia. The decision to leave Worcestershire and English county cricket was not taken lightly. Indeed it was a regretful parting, the end of a long chapter in my life, but I always had a secret fear of overstaying my usefulness in the first-class game. I wanted to go when I would still be remembered as a batsman of some ability, and not for what I used to be before I slipped down the wrong side of the hill.

Don Kenyon's decline had served as a warning to me. Don was my senior by three years, and I had always had the highest regard for his ability. In my view he was one of the game's outstanding openers, but tragically he reached a point when he was scarcely worth his place in the side. I vowed, as I approached my fortieth birthday, that time would not similarly cheat me.

At the end of the 1970 season Jackie and I sold up everything, and went on an assisted passage to Brisbane, accompanied by our son Tim, then only ten, and our daughter Becky, who was sixteen. I had accepted in my mind that we were going for good, an opinion reinforced by the warmth with which we were feted on our arrival.

The skies were cloudless, our hopes were high. No sooner had our first task of finding a house been completed than Jackie, who had had jaundice twice in the past, fell ill, and she was in hospital during one of the most miserable and anxious Christmases the family have known – a wretched start to life 'down under'.

While awaiting our furniture, the children and I lived in a motel. Tim went to the Church of England Grammar School, settling in with all the adaptability of his age, and Becky did extremely well at a secretarial college. Eventually she became secretary to the greyhound racing manager with the Brisbane Cricket Ground Trust, and my only complaint was that the dogs never seemed to have heard of the hot inside information which came my way! As a tipster Becky was a splendid secretary.

One of my first games for Queensland was against England, but Ken Shuttleworth bowled me for four in a strange match which never got beyond an innings apiece. Sam Trimble, the Queensland captain, seemed determined to prove a point, and he batted for nine hours and scored 177. Sam didn't declare and Queensland went into the third afternoon. Then

I fielded while MCC (as they were then) made 418 for 4, with
Geoff Boycott scoring 124 and John Edrich 120.

Trimble was one of the heaviest scorers in Australia's
domestic cricket, but although he toured the West Indies he
never had a Test. Queensland, during his captaincy, was the
unfashionable cricket state, its team regarded as the banana
benders and fifteen years behind the rest of Australia. Perhaps his tactics against England represented a cry from the
heart, but understandably they were not appreciated by Ray
Illingworth and Co.

It was, I have to admit, something of an odd experience to
be pitted against my old mates. And odder still to be in a side
which not only failed to win a match all season, but failed
even to get a first-innings lead. Queensland were firmly
anchored at the bottom of the Sheffield Shield league.

My last appearance for Queensland came in November
1971, when I was rushed to Melbourne from Brisbane to
captain the team in place of the injured Trimble. True to
Queensland's fortunes at the time, I lost the toss and we were
trapped on a difficult pitch and lost by an innings. I finished
21 not out in the second innings as I ran out of partners.

From the start I had impressed on Clem Jones that I
regarded myself more as a coach than a player, but he wanted
me to stay in the side. Finally it became almost a physical
impossibility for me at that stage of my cricket life. Queensland had a weak side with little bowling, and it became an
ordeal to field for long stretches on the vast outfields, rock
hard on the soles of the feet, and in temperatures around 100
degrees.

The only innings to give me true satisfaction was a 98 in a
knock-out game at Adelaide, which earned me the Man of the
Match award. As Jackie was still in hospital and I needed to
get back to Brisbane as fast as I could, I had no time to stay
and collect my medal from Sir Donald Bradman.

It did not take me long to discover that Clem Jones was
not only the city mayor, and involved in any number of
activities, but was to all intents and purposes the dictator of

Queensland cricket. He was prodigious in his efforts and support for cricket, and later it came as no surprise to me to learn that he had sacked the groundsman and had himself taken on the preparation of the pitch for the first Test during England's visit in 1974-5. The weather took a hand, and forty-eight hours before the start the square looked like the mud beach at Southend after the tide had gone out. After spending days with a trowel smoothing out the mud, Clem contrived a pitch of sorts, which cost England dear with injuries and a defeat.

Though we had a lovely home, and Brisbane has many delights to savour, not least the sunshine, it became increasingly clear that I did not measure up to Jones' expectations of me. In retrospect, I think I was too old for Australian-style combat on the field, and it niggled Jones that he had chosen a man who, as he saw it, could not deliver the goods.

My contract had been for three years, but it ended after two with a minor squabble, which suddenly assumed major importance. I had arrived at the ground early in order to contact Ernie Toovey, the chairman of selectors, to discuss the colts team, due to play in Sydney. I told Fay, Clem's secretary, that I intended to use his office to make this call, as it would be secluded and away from the noise of typewriters and callers in the outer office.

No sooner had I put the call through than Jones stormed into the room and, as he tried to whisk the phone from my hands, demanded, 'What right have you to use my room, my desk and my telephone?' My right, as I saw it, was that it was in the service of Queensland cricket, and I objected to being treated in that high-handed authoritative manner, as if I were of no account.

The row ended with my stalking out of the room and slamming the door in his face - admittedly not the most tactful of gestures. Still steamed up, I contacted Norman McMahon, the chairman, to tell him that I wanted to end my association and to return to England at the first available opportunity. None of the state officials seemed to worry all that much about the sudden break. Nor did I, though I sincerely regretted parting with the likes of Ray Lindwall, the late Ken ('Slasher') Mackay and Ron Archer.

We had marvellous times together, which only those who have experienced the friendship of old cricketers can understand. I had also made a firm friend in Lou Cooper, the secretary of Queensland Cricket Association, who had been partly instrumental in my appointment. But he had his own problems and left the job.

Clem Jones was a hard taskmaster, but I do not think even he could have been displeased with my coaching at schoolboy level, which was close to my heart. Not only was there fanatical enthusiasm, but some were comfortably the best I have seen in the eleven-year-old age group. The standard of junior cricket in Queensland had to be seen to be believed, and it remained high until the boys were old enough to hold a driving licence and impress a girlfriend with their prowess on a surfboard. I often thought cricket should be a winter game in Queensland, for under scorching suns in high temperatures much of the keenness is roasted out of them.

Another reason for our decision to quit Australia was the fact that my business activities hardly flourished. After travelling 1,200 miles up the coast to Cairns, a big mining area, I became involved with Mineral Securities, but, far from yielding a fortune, they went bust. My other efforts in insurance did no better.

Queensland's state side were also in the doldrums. Among my pupils were John MacLean, who under-studied the Test wicket-keeper Rodney Marsh, and the all-rounder Carlson, who promised much but never quite made it.

In my time Queensland were a poor team at a transitional stage, having yet to recover from the retirements of Ken MacKay, Ron Archer and Peter Burge. Peter introduced me to the Albion Park Trotting Track, which, though another excuse for losing money, was great fun. My companionship of the older players was alone well worth the venture. Though my stay ended in acrimonious circumstances, I would not have missed it for anything, and I was delighted when Queensland's fortunes picked up with the arrival of Greg Chappell from South Australia. Greg always looked on me as his lucky talisman, because on the few occasions I played against him he always scored runs.

Returning to England, almost broke, I had an offer to play for Derbyshire, but I was not attracted, as I thought I could help Worcestershire by turning out in a few Second XI matches. To my acute disappointment I was not impressed by what I saw. The spirit was not there, and I finished by telling a fast bowler that he was not putting his heart into his work. Naturally he did not enjoy being told a home truth, and I reluctantly decided it was a waste of time working with players who were not prepared to give everything to the game and improve their skills.

An alternative might have been to link up with a local club, but I still had an itch to bat as long as I could, and I was scared of depriving a deserving youngster of an innings for which he has waited all week! And so I drifted out of the game.

I also had a nine-month spell at a squash club at Westcliff-on-Sea, and there was a vague suggestion that I might have some games for Essex. Wisely, neither Essex nor I pursued the idea!

7
Tours, Tantrums and Tear Gas

I captained England one and a half times, the half being in 1968 when I took over from Colin Cowdrey mid-way through the third Test against Bill Lawry's Australians at Edgbaston. Cowdrey went lame during his twenty-first century in his hundredth Test, a record number of appearances at the time. By an unhappy coincidence Bill Lawry broke a finger, and the acting captains were Graveney and Graham McKenzie, the genial fast bowler who spent some seasons with Leicestershire.

Few generals would want to assume command in the thick of battle, and in a sense it is much the same on the cricket field. There is a responsibility not to lose an advantage previously gained, and clearly it is no time to put personal theories to the test. A holding operation is expected.

Yet I had my moment to defy convention of the time and use the two spinners, Ray Illingworth and Derek Underwood. They grabbed five wickets and Australia only just escaped the follow-on. *Wisden* commented that most people were surprised by England's positive approach.

With Cowdrey still unfit I retained the captaincy for the fourth Test at Headingley. Events conspired against me even before the start. I had a deep and nasty hand wound, which would make slip fielding impossible, so the selectors sent for Phil Sharpe, who they knew was about to open the Yorkshire innings at Westcliffe. Indeed, he was already at the wicket.

England had fourteen players, including Cowdrey on stand-by, and to the disappointment of the Yorkshire crowd, who can seldom be accused of impartiality in such matters, Keith Fletcher was given his first cap instead of Sharpe.

Poor Fletcher, at first slip, made three gallant but vain efforts to take low and wide snicks. The crowd were convinced that they would have been caught by Sharpe, a brilliant slip specialist, and Fletcher was unfairly made a scapegoat. Subsequently he looked forward to visits to Headingley with the relish of an old lag appearing at the Old Bailey. Years later he was even barracked during net practice the day before a Test. Tony Greig, the England captain, angrily turned on one man with the question: 'Just whose side are you on?'

One of my problems was Australia's clear policy to avoid defeat and retain the Ashes on the strength of their victory in the first Test at Old Trafford. To make it more difficult, the pitch was playing low and slow after much rain. Australia dug in during their second innings, and inevitably there was a generally sour condemnation of events.

I did not escape criticism, but fortunately there was a different assessment behind the scenes. Freddie Brown, whose judgement I would accept before that of some of the critics, told me: 'You did a super job and everybody who played under you said how much they enjoyed it.'

Brown's reassuring words and my selection as vice-captain to Cowdrey for the rescheduled tour that winter suggested that I might be in line of succession for the job every cricketer covets – to lead his country. But the Graveney luck ran out during the next shambling months. After the South African tour was abandoned it was planned to go to India and Pakistan, but India pulled out on financial grounds and MCC were left with Pakistan and twelve days in Sri Lanka – or Ceylon, as it was then.

Sri Lanka proved to be the relaxing calm before the storm. While we were in Colombo, amid the palm trees and tea plantations and working elephants – an idyll enhanced for me by a century in the representative match against All Ceylon

– disturbing reports reached us of civil disorders in Pakistan. We didn't know the half of it. Not to put too fine a point on it, Pakistan was in a state of simmering violence, the first evidence of which was the sight of armed soldiers lining the streets on the journey from airport to hotel.

If either the politicians or the cricket authorities had been possessed of common sense, or feeling for the players, the tour would have been called off there and then. Instead cricket was seized upon as a unifying element, and became a political pawn. The odd feature was that though public assemblies were forbidden, crowds were allowed to gather at cricket grounds. The opportunity to express feelings and demonstrate was not passed by.

The first Test at Lahore was constantly disrupted. There was scarcely a session without invasions of the pitch by rioting students. Cricket was the backcloth and rallying-point for the agitators from various political factions. A less tranquil personality than the manager Leslie Ames would have been driven mad. The British High Commissions were most concerned with 'Pak–Bri relations' (how many times did we hear those words!) and the home authorities gave bland assurances they were in no position to honour. At one stage the team were confined to the Inter-Continental Hotel at Lahore, and the days were idly spent on a pitch and putt course.

Roger Prideaux, the captain of Northamptonshire, sneaked out to give a trial to a young student bowler by the name of Sarfraz Nawaz at the nearby Indian Gymkhana Club. In what surely must have been the most bizarre trial ever conducted on behalf of an English county, Sarfraz Nawaz bowled behind barbed wire while armed soldiers surrounded the net.

Meanwhile the manager had received a signal concerning the situation in East Pakistan, now Bangladesh, where the second Test was due to be played at the capital Dacca. While the politicians argued and manoeuvred, Dacca was on, off and on again. Understandably the manager and captain were very concerned about the reported disturbances at Dacca, and the three of us left Sahiwal, where the match had been called off because of rain, for an emergency meeting with the members of the Pakistan Board of Control. In political jargon we had a frank and full discussion, but the Board had received a telegram from the British High Commission at Dacca to say that, if MCC did not go, all the High Commission buildings and property would be burnt down by the mob. We were also assured that the team would have the full protection of the police, and the Army would be on hand. There would be no problems on that score, and, accordingly, there was no sound argument against our going.

When we arrived at Dacca Airport, the manager, the captain and I were taken in the Commissioner's car to the Inter-Continental Hotel. All seemed peaceful enough, but there was a marked absence of police. I asked the obvious question: 'I can't see any police. Where are they?' The reply was: 'Well, the Army are camped ten miles out, and the only police in the city are traffic police. The city is being run by the local students.' Some of our confidence abruptly disappeared.

Before the Test started we had a meeting with four students, the eldest of whom could not have been more than twenty, who were deciding whether they should allow the match to take place! Remarkably the students were indeed in control and they guaranteed that there would be no trouble and that the England players had nothing to fear. Behind his amiable manner Les Ames is a tough character, and as he did his best to put the genuine fears of the players to rest, he was all for flying the flag and going through with the fixture whatever happened.

I cannot believe there has been a stranger pre-Test meeting in the history of cricket and, looking back, in the cold light of reason and distance, I need to pinch myself to believe it really did take place.

As it turned out Dacca was by far the least interrupted of the three Test matches – Karachi in fact had to be abandoned because of constant rioting – and such was the status of the students that there were no police on the ground. Colin

Cowdrey, who had his wallet taken by a pickpocket when crossing the width of a pavement from team coach to the ground entrance, was the only victim.

I could have been another casualty in another astonishing incident of a different kind involving John Snow, England's main strike bowler. In Sri Lanka, Snow, a truly magnificent bowler but given to unpredictable moods, had not exactly exhibited burning zeal, and the selectors – Cowdrey, Ames, John Edrich and myself – left him out of the opening Test and gave Bob Cottam his first chance for England. In fairness the combination of heat and humidity has a debilitating effect on bowlers in Colombo, but Snow had taken only five wickets in the two and a bit matches – only twenty-five overs had been completed at Sahiwal – in Pakistan.

Snow was restored for the Dacca Test and when I, vice-captain and selector, went in to bat in the nets, I looked up and saw him in the far distance using, I imagine, his full run for the first time on the tour. A few warning bells rang in my suspicious mind and, sure enough, the first ball was a bouncer which struck me on my top hand. Whether or not it was bowled in a fit of pique, whether he felt he had a personal point to make, is not for me to say, but it was a stupid thing to do as we had only six batsmen and, as Cowdrey's fitness was in doubt, we had felt obliged to send for Colin Milburn from Western Australia. (I don't think Colin Milburn ever forgave us because he had been due to share a cabin on the ship to England with Graham McKenzie – a guarantee of social success.)

I suppose I took eighteen or nineteen balls from Snow, of which sixteen or seventeen were bouncers. At least I knew what was coming and, as the wicket was fairly easy-paced, I was able to get into position and polish up my hooking. At the end of the net I said my customary 'Thank you' to the bowlers, including 'Snowie', when I was joined by Les Ames. 'What on earth's been going on?' he indignantly demanded. 'I almost got up from my seat and sent him home after his fifth bouncer.' Les is a man slow to anger, and he was certainly angry then, for England wanted Snow as a bowler and not as a secret weapon for Pakistan.

Later Ames said I handled the incident in the right way by carrying on and having hooking practice.

That was John Snow, the self-confessed cricket rebel. You never quite knew what he was going to do. When we were in the West Indies in 1967–68, Cowdrey and I watched him from the balcony in the first match, being hit all over Bridgetown by Colts batsmen who, in truth, were very ordinary performers. Cowdrey sighed and said despondently, 'I think he's going to be a waste of time on this trip.' As it turned out Snow proved to be the fastest and most dangerous bowler on either side and, with 27 wickets, was the most potent factor in England's victory, just as he was later to be in Australia under Ray Illingworth.

At his best Snow was right up to the lofty standard set by the best of England's post-war fast bowlers. In county matches he never held anything back against me, and we had some real ding-dong battles. As far as I am aware I did not give him cause for the 'special treatment', except that it is as natural for fast bowlers to get at batsmen as it is for dogs to chase cats. Middlesex's John Price was another to bowl flat out to me, which I always accepted as a compliment. Snow and, to a lesser extent, Price would bowl like a demon at the first five in the order, and sometimes like a clown at the tail-enders. Perhaps they lost interest, or were less attracted to picking up easy wickets. I doubt whether even Snow could give the answer.

I looked on Snow's back break, the good length 'nip backer', as his deadliest delivery, particularly early on, and accordingly I tried to get on to my front foot. As he knew precisely what I had in mind, he invariably welcomed me with a bouncer. A lot of fast bowlers followed his tactics, and the older I got, and the slower my reactions, the more I tried to get on to the front foot until I had acclimatised and picked up the pace of the pitch.

★   ★   ★

From Dacca, where the game was inevitably drawn, we went to Karachi for the third and final Test. There had been no improvement in law and order, and many of the England players looked to me to put their case to the authorities. There was no question that they were terrified of taking the field and being exposed to the whims and capricious conduct of scheming agitators seeking a platform for demonstrations denied them in the streets. I firmly believed, and events were to prove me right, that the players were not over-reacting or over-dramatising the situation, and they had every right to fear being manhandled. Even their lives were being put at risk, for it needed only one maniac in an uncontrolled mob to go berserk with a knife. Because I shared the alarm and was a senior player, I became the team's spokesman. I think it was to cost me dear.

Karachi was potentially the most dangerous of the Test centres. As soon as we arrived for the Test the tour management sought another discussion with the Pakistan Board of Control and, as before, the air was full of glib promises that all was under control and there was no cause for misgivings.

But patently everything was not under control, as the previous six weeks in Pakistan had shown, and finally, after one smooth talker had turned facts upside down, I lost my temper. I regret to say I swore and finally retired to a corner with the words: 'Right, you make your own arrangements. I know what I know and what the England team thinks.' What the team thought is not publishable. But, apart from the ambition to return home in one piece, there was a general feeling that they had been kicked around long enough by authority in one guise or another for ends other than cricket.

Les Ames and Colin Cowdrey nobly stuck to their 'fly the flag' policy. Fair enough – and but for them the situation would have undoubtedly been far, far worse – but I have since felt that my outburst may have had a bearing on the events which followed a few months later when Cowdrey snapped an achilles tendon and the England captaincy was thrown open.

Our delegation left the meeting with the Board with promises of this and that, and I thought it would be a miracle if they could be fulfilled. The miracle was not achieved, and early on the third morning the Test was abandoned after the most serious of the many interruptions which had plagued the match from the start.

I was batting during some of the pitch invasions, and I can testify just how terrifying an experience it can be to be surrounded by howling fanatics. There you are in the centre of a huge stadium when suddenly, for no apparent reason, you see hordes of running figures, some screeching with excitement, approaching from every direction. The first instinctive reaction is annoyance that one's concentration has been broken. The second is to wonder if it is one of those mindless interruptions from exhibitionists which have become fashionable, or whether it is politically motivated. The third is to measure the distance between the crease and the dressing-room, and how fast one can run in pads!

When Majid Khan, playing against England for the first time, reached his 50 in the Lahore Test, scores of spectators jumped the fences and engulfed their hero, who ended at the bottom of a heap of bodies. England's fielders had to pile in and throw young men aside in order to rescue Majid, who was in danger of being suffocated.

At Karachi I batted with Colin Milburn, who sadly was never to bat again for England. His car accident and the loss of an eye in May was a profound tragedy for him, England and Northamptonshire just as he was reaching his jubilant prime. Colin scored two centuries for England and I batted with him on both occasions – against the West Indies at Lord's and here at Karachi. Colin made 139 and I had 105, and we took the total from 78 to 234 for 2.

When I went in at the fall of John Edrich's wicket, Milburn was going like a bomb, and his century was greeted by a mass surge to the middle. In no time he was surrounded. In his defence I started flailing my bat, but it did not seem to matter if I hit anybody. I was determined he should not be hurled to the ground and possibly injured, and I circled round his considerable girth holding spectators at bay and yelling, 'Get off the pitch, you're not supposed to be here.' Fortunately the police arrived in support and Colin was not further molested.

And so it went on for two days, with the authorities facing what seemed to be an insoluble dilemma. On the one side, it was argued that it was necessary to have police around the ground inside the perimeter to stop spectators running on to the pitch; on the other, it was insisted that the presence of the police was a provocation answered by the throwing of oranges and any missile to hand. A fifteen-foot-high wire fence was no barrier. One of the saddest side-effects of the continuing violence, caused mainly by wild youngsters, was that it drove the genuine cricket-lover away – as has happened with our own soccer.

The final riot caused the match to be abandoned on the third morning when Alan Knott, then without a Test century, was 96 not out. I remember his forlorn remark as he cast his eyes heavenward: 'Someone up there can't like me.'

Those at the highest point in the stadium speak of seeing a mob approaching like an invading army, short only of battering-rams. In no time they broke down the gates and tore the ground apart. Tents and awnings went up in flames, and the stumps were smashed. As I saw the remains of a stump battered in half and looked at the thickness of the wood, I wondered what kind of violence could have caused it. The mind boggled. Troops arrived with 'one up the spout', and the players were locked in the dressing-rooms for at least an hour.

England's coach came at last and as we got in the stones began flying through the air. I remember seeing the expression of dazed incredulity on Keith Fletcher's face. Our players were yelling to the driver, 'Let's get out of here.' As someone remarked: 'Cricket, lovely, Cricket.'

There have been so many crowd interruptions at Karachi

over the years that there is a good case for banning the ground as a Test centre.

Late that evening we left on what we had happily thought was to be a half-filled plane, but, as we prepared to stretch out in reasonable comfort, a poker-faced Chinese trade delegation, dressed identically in the familiar tunics, marched down the gangway and took all the remaining seats. The trip to Paris was certainly not in the luxury class, but by then most of the team would have gladly volunteered to be strapped to a wing to return home.

Robin Hobbs was the one member of the England party entitled to have a private chuckle at the whole affair. The averages reveal that he played in one Test but he did not bat or bowl. Perhaps it was just as well. On the whole tour of Sri Lanka and Pakistan, Robin bowled only twenty overs for two wickets and never once went to the wicket. Understandably he never dreamt he would be called up for the Karachi Test, that final match, so he had disposed of his kit. Cricket gear was in short supply in Pakistan at the time, and players were constantly asked for spare bats, pads, gloves – in fact anything in a bag.

Feeling that he had no further use for them, he got rid of the lot. Then Colin Cowdrey decided he would like a leg spinner at Karachi, and Hobbs was in. Hastily he begged and borrowed, but as Number 11 he merely had to sit and watch England reach 502 for 7 before the final disruption ended the game.

Robin has a great sense of humour. I would for instance like to know what he thought of being recruited by Glamorgan as captain after his days with Essex were over.

Wisden's verdict after the Pakistan misadventure, that I was a disappointment and was more suited to the role of first mate than captain, surprised me as I had not had any opportunity to be in charge. Surely an assessment can only be properly made *after* a spell of leadership. Without trying too hard, I can think of several captains who were not startling successes after being the darlings of the critics; and others, who were looked on doubtfully, who did well as county captains. You can't judge the taste of a cake until it's been eaten.

Test captains need to have a tough streak. Hutton's single-minded attitude was brought home to me in a manner which made me smile in the midst of the first riot I saw – at the fourth Test at Georgetown in 1954. England had lost the first two Tests and, with the next ending in a predictable draw on the Trinidad mat, Hutton knew he had to win to have any chance of saving the series.

Bottles and boxes and the like were thrown when Cliff McWatt, a local hero, went for what would have been the hundredth run of a partnership with J.K. Holt. Peter May ran him out by a considerable distance – at least two or three yards, on the batsman's admission. Again, whether it was a planned political disruption or came through a combination of rum, betting and disappointment, was a matter of guess-work. Play was held up for ten minutes while the players watched the débris pile up. Johnny Wardle pretended to take a swig from a bottle and feigned drunkenness to try and pacify the crowd, but finally W.S. Jones, then President of the local Board of Control, left the pavilion to speak to Hutton.

'The scene is becoming ugly,' said de Santos. 'Senior officials think you and your team should come off the field.'

I was close at hand with Sonny Ramadhin, one of the batsmen, and we heard Hutton reply, 'No, we'll stay. These people are not going to get us off. That might be their idea, but if so, they are wrong. We mean to win the match and I want another wicket or two this evening.'

Whereupon Ramadhin said, 'Well you can have mine if you want it.'

On the resumption Ramadhin was immediately bowled by Jim Laker, missing the first straight delivery bowled to him, and departed with undisguised alacrity. Hutton, who had made 169, duly forced the follow-on and we won by nine wickets in what MCC prudently referred to as 'difficult circumstances' in a congratulatory telegram.

In the match against British Guiana (as it was then) Willie Watson and I put on 402 for the fourth wicket and, if we had not been given instructions to get out and give others some batting practice, notably Sussex's Ken Suttle, I think we could have broken every record in the book. At Number 5 after Hutton, May and Compton, I had resigned myself to a long wait, but Hutton was out for a 'duck', May scored 9 and Compton 18. When he came in Len said, 'You'll never have a better wicket to bat on and more ordinary bowling.'

All I remember is that Willie, who hit 257, and I (231) just kept hitting boundaries. Among the eight bowlers tried was a young off-spinner named Lance Gibbs, but he made no impression on me at that time.

Sabina Park, Jamaica, was the scene of more crowd incidents on Cowdrey's 1967-8 tour. The worst and most worrying feature was that it almost cost England the match when they had been in a winning position. West Indies were in deep trouble when Basil Butcher was caught down the leg side by Jim Parks off Basil D'Oliveira. There was no question that he was out. Butcher, a very fair cricketer, did not even wait to be given out and departed as soon as he saw the ball go into the wicket-keeper's gloves. As he walked off, however, the bottles began to fly, and out came the riot squad complete with shields.

Cowdrey, Sir Gary Sobers, who was batting, and I went to try and calm the crowd. 'Come on,' we said, 'that was fair enough.' The reply we had was a depressing 'Ah yes, but if it had been Cowdrey or you you wouldn't have been given out.' Frankly there is no point in arguing with such crass bigotry. And if Gary could not get a hearing, what chance had we? As we gave up and started for the pavilion a bottle hit the police inspector in charge of the riot squad.

'Tear gas!' he promptly roared. The wind, however, was blowing in the wrong direction, away from the rioters and straight into the pavilion. We put wet handkerchiefs over our steaming eyes like gas-assaulted soldiers of the First World War. Absolute chaos. Then, on reflection, England made a major mistake by agreeing to resume play shortly after the fracas. Nobody could honestly say their concentration was on cricket. We were wondering if something else would happen, and the West Indies got off the hook. To make up for the time lost during the interruption it was agreed to add an extra seventy-five minutes. To my mind that was absolutely crazy, because the victims, in this instance England, had to bear the brunt of the consequences of the interruption.

As it was, England won a run-chase at Port-of-Spain and took the series.

One of Ted Dexter's less inspired ideas was to invite the athlete Gordon Pirie, a fellow passenger on the *Canberra* en route to Australia in 1962, to supervise the team's daily morning keep fit session. The idea was to run round the deck for the equivalent of a three-mile jog. Soon Pirie was in splendid isolation. Brian Statham and I would complete a lap and a half and disappear down one of the centre hatchways. My conscience was clear as, after a hard season scoring more than 2,000 runs (which in itself represented a fair amount of running), I needed the voyage to re-charge my batteries.

Freddie Truman was not impressed by the new methods, and promised, 'If I ever catch up with that man Pirie, someone will be shouting "man overboard" and it won't be me.'

Arriving in Australia, Pirie described us as the unfittest set of sportmen he had ever come across, which was patently absurd. Cricketers need to pace themselves over a longer period than is necessary in other sports, and I am not quite sure of the value of the modern practice of lapping the ground before a day's play. If a player is not fit, then he ought not to be in the team. The time for running is after a net practice. The fifteen-minute gymnastic display now to be seen would not have suited me or many of my contemporaries, who were able to bat for longer periods than seems possible in the eighties, and thought nothing of bowling thirty-odd overs during the course of a day. Nowadays, for all the attention to fitness, there are more injuries than in my day, and bowlers have broken down with startling frequency. When I was at Worcester the professional footballers in the side like Jim Standen and Ted Hemsley admitted that a day in the field wore them out until they became attuned to the special needs of cricket, which include constant concentration as well as agility and stamina.

I believe Dexter was rather stifled by the promise of positive attacking cricket, made with rash fervour, and by the presence of the Duke of Norfolk as manager. Not that the Duke was anything but a genuine cricket-lover, pleasant and even retiring, but the Aussies were intrigued by having a real live Duke as manager and perhaps expected too much. Much of the attention was on the Duke rather than Dexter and his team, and the situation was made unreal when he returned home to attend a rehearsal for a State occasion, and Billy Griffith, then MCC secretary, flew out as a replacement. A lot of extra work fell on Alec Bedser as assistant manager. Dexter must have been a little bemused, even if he did not admit it. In 1957 I went with the Duke's private team to Jamaica, and I knew what to expect. In fact he was a little shy of Test cricketers, strange as it may seem.

Even before the tour there had been a summer of argument over the captaincy, a tug of war between Dexter and Cowdrey, with the Rev. David Sheppard, now the Anglican Bishop of Liverpool, making a come-back and also entering the lists. If one read some newspapers it seemed as if the position had been half-promised to Sheppard and was clinched by a century for the Gentlemen against the Players. But Dexter was named. I think David would have been a more logical captain in Australia and easier for the players to work with. He was more straightforward in his approach than Dexter, but, I admit, he was not seriously tested in the one Test I had under him in the home series with Pakistan in 1954.

He was still reading for holy orders when he was called –

if that be the right word – to take over for two Tests when Len Hutton was taken ill. Two years later he became the first ordained priest to play in Test cricket, and I was amused to hear the passing words of two Australians, who presumably were Roman Catholics. One said, 'If he was in our mob he'd be a bishop by now!'

On his second tour of Australia, David's 113 in the Melbourne Test was the largest single contribution to England's victory, but, sadly, he had lost his great ability as a close-to-the-wicket catcher. Gradually he was banished further and further away from the wicket, but the catches still would not stick. Once, when a comfortable chance went down, Freddie Trueman, the bowler, stood glowering, hands on hips, in the middle of the pitch. For a moment I was fearful of what might come out, but Freddie rose to the occasion magnificently. 'If the reverend gentleman cannot put his hands together, what ruddy hope is there for the rest of us?' he growled.

At last David held a catch when Bill Lawry hooked Barry Knight high to long-leg. Delightedly he threw the ball high in the air, so high in fact that Lawry and Bobby Simpson stole a second run. Alas for poor David, he had not heard the cry of 'No ball'.

Most assessments of David's ability suggest that he was something of a 'made' cricketer, but I do not go along with that view at all. If anything, David was too orthodox, which meant that a field could confidently be set against him. Sir Don Bradman once made this point, and in fact it was true – many of David's shots going direct to a fielder. It may be said that he intelligently made the maximum use of his natural talent, but that is another thing altogether. David's record, which included three Test centuries – two against Australia – and 2,262 runs in the season he topped the national averages, proves his considerable ability. If the Church had not claimed him I am sure he would have filled an England opening position for many years to come – not to mention the captaincy.

I remember a gesture he made to the late Frank Lee, a very fair and conscientious umpire. David was dismissed just before play was stopped for bad light at Old Trafford. As Frank came in David was waiting to assure him that the light had nothing to do with his getting out.

8
Colleagues at the Crease

The three great English batsmen in my playing days were Sir Len Hutton, the master of every technique, Denis Compton, whose natural, irreducible genius made a joke of every coaching book, and Peter May, one of the most brilliant exponents of back-play cricket has known.

At the next level of the very good to the good came Colin Cowdrey, Ken Barrington, Ted Dexter, John Edrich, Geoff Boycott and, if I may be allowed to depart from modesty, myself. It was a group which ranged from Cowdrey, who did not make the maximum use of his ability, to Edrich, who did because he was a practical character with a heart as big as a balloon.

Cowdrey had the talent to be at least as good as May, who must remain the best product of the post-war era – Hutton and Compton having started for England in 1937. To those of us privileged to be present when Cowdrey scored his first Test century at Melbourne in 1954-5 he remains forever a particular enigma. On a pitch which defeated Hutton, Bill Edrich, May and Compton on the first morning, Colin, then twenty-two and in his third Test, scored 50 out of 69 and 100 out of 158 against bowlers of the calibre of Lindwall, Miller, Ron Archer, Benaud, Bill Johnston and Ian Johnson. Here was unbridled genius, and I need to dig deep into the well of memory to try and recall an innings of such merit and technique. Having done so, I don't think I can!

Yet I, in common with the rest who watched him with rising excitement, have since wondered why he never played as well again. At least I never saw a comparable performance, though I acknowledge several innings of the highest quality. He remained an enigma. I have never been able to understand why a batsman who could play at his Melbourne level, even if only once in his career, should want to fiddle around with the weight of his bat, change his grip, be bothered by the way he held his bat and so on. Surely there was no cause for him to fuss about with technical experiments like an ordinary player feeling his way. There was no need to change. With talent like his, proved in the infant days of his Test career, you stay as you are. You just go out and play, and thank the good Lord above for bestowing gifts not given to ordinary mortals.

In twenty-five years of first-class cricket I had my ups and downs, but once I had discovered an inner confidence I never altered my grip – though possibly I gripped a little tighter with my top hand when I became fractionally on-side in my play – my pick-up, the weight of my bat, or even added a second rubber to the handle. I never believed in interfering with the basics once they had been shown to be right.

If Cowdrey had matched May's steel he would have been at least his equal, and it is not possible to offer higher praise. Barrington and Boycott were eye-catching stroke players when they first started, but became stockpilers of runs and, again, stifled their own talent. Had they given full expression to their innate talent I think they could have been even better.

Boycott developed a fetish about not getting out. On one occasion he made an astounding statement: 'My job's to see the shine off the ball.' And left it at that. For a player of his talent to reduce his art to one mundane everyday responsibility, albeit important enough as an opener, is nothing short of ridiculous. A Boycott letting himself go would have numbered among the immortals. As it is, the mere accumulation of runs is a contribution to statistics and not evidence of greatness. Hutton, Compton, May, Bradman, Graeme Pollock, Weekes, Worrell and Walcott stand apart because they won matches; they took over Tests with the bat; they dominated. They imposed their will over bowlers of all types, and to my mind, well as he has played, Boycott too often fell short of that essential hallmark of greatness.

Boycott has been a victim of a self-imposed bondage, and his own complex moods. At one point he dropped out of Test cricket for three years, and then, after displaying honourable loyalty to the establishment during the Packer crisis, he went off to South Africa on an unofficial tour in defiance of that same authority and clobbered a three-year Test ban. Whatever the rights and wrongs of the latter dispute and the justice, or otherwise, of the ban, it was part of his illogical pattern of behaviour which is so hard to understand.

The carryings-on over the captaincy at Yorkshire were equally complex and, to the outsiders like myself, looked like a family squabble which should have been avoidable. I know what it is like to be kicked out of the captaincy at county level, and I sympathised, but after eight years without tangible success Boycott had no divine right to the job. If he felt as strongly as he apparently did, he should have taken a leaf out of my book and left with as much dignity as he could muster, started afresh with a new club, and made up his mind to enjoy what was left of his playing career.

Yorkies have a different approach to cricket from most of us, which is not an implied criticism but a fact, as I discovered playing under Hutton who, as captain, earned all the praise and deserved some of the criticism to come his way.

Twice when I was his partner – admittedly very much the junior partner – in crucial phases of Test matches, he stopped me from playing my natural game. One particular shot of mine, I am sure, did lead him to believe that I could not play cricket, at least not in the Hutton way.

The occasion was at Lord's in 1953 when we took the total from nine for the loss of Don Kenyon's wicket to 177, then England's best post-war stand against Australia. Big Bill Johnston, that superb left-arm support to Lindwall and

Miller, came in from the pavilion end when I was well set in the mid-twenties. The ball was a half-volley which started to swing and continued to swing away from me. As I was already committed on the front foot instinctively I hit it with a flat bat square and it went to the Grand Stand boundary like a rocket. I had never played a shot like it in my life, and as I hit it, and it sped from the bat, I laughed and looked down the wicket.

The expression on Len's face was one of sheer stupefaction. 'What's on?' he asked. 'I've never played a shot like that before,' I replied, and for a moment I envisaged myself summoned before the full MCC committee to answer a charge of playing a blasphemous stroke! An unpardonable dereliction of duty.

Delighted as I was to play a part in a recovery, as I had done with Hutton in the previous Test at Trent Bridge, it had to be unfortunate that Len should come to me some forty minutes or so before the close and caution me with the words: 'We don't want to lose another wicket tonight.' That was, in effect, an order and I have since read that all the scoring strokes were locked away in the last hour. A fair criticism, as by then the Aussies, if not wilting, had had enough for that day and had lost the sharp edge of their aggression. I felt there were runs for the taking, whether it was the last hour or not, but the instructions of the captain had to be obeyed. As we batted out to the close for a few frugal runs I had a suspicion that we were passing over an opportunity. So it proved to be.

The following morning Lindwall, still using the old ball, slipped in his famous in-swinging yorker with his third delivery – the very type of ball I had steeled myself to expect and guard against. Even so I was unlucky. I actually hit the ball hard enough to leave a solid mark on my bat a good quarter of an inch up from the bottom in the centre. Yet it still got through to bowl me.

Ray and I are close friends, and while talking over old times as old players do, he has assured me it was one of the best yorkers he ever bowled – a point on which I am not prepared to argue!

I cannot conceive it possible that in the whole history of cricket there has been a better fast bowler than Raymond Russell Lindwall, whose action was poetry in motion and who promoted quick bowling into an art form. Merely to talk to him is an education, and a laughable indictment of the old belief that brawn and not brain is the first requisite of pace. Not that Ray was anything but the fittest athlete imaginable.

First, he acquired such an encyclopaedic knowledge of the strengths and weaknesses of the major batsmen that his brain responded like a computer to a programmer as soon as a newcomer arrived at the crease. Second, by intuition and subtle probing, he knew almost straight away if they were in form. If so, he would shrewdly bowl within himself, though still quick enough for discomfort, and bide his time in a cat-and-mouse type of exercise. Just when the batsman was starting to think this was going to be his day, Ray would suddenly unloose a thunderbolt at top speed. It could be an in-swinger (developed in the Lancashire League), an out-swinger, his stock ball when I first saw him in 1948, a swinging yorker to dart in like a snake, or a bumper calling for hurried evasive action. His barely detectable changes of pace might have come from Derek Underwood, and he always had superb control and accuracy.

His away-swinger, helped by his lowish action, moved like a boomerang. Indeed it swung so far that the number of batsmen bowled off-stump, playing toward mid-on, was legion. Many's the time he out-thought the most canny and experienced of top international batsmen, and he never stopped expanding and developing his bowling. He was the complete fast bowler.

The other occasion when Hutton clipped my wings was at Barbados, in 1954, on the day which came to be known as

Black Tuesday. England's output in five and a half hours on a perfect batting pitch was 128 runs from 114 overs and, worse still, for the loss of seven wickets. Len's strategy was to defend and let the runs come, a policy as popular in the West Indies as Communism in the United States. Having lost the first Test at Sabina Park, Kingston, Hutton's chief worry was the spin combination of Sonny Ramadhin and Alf Valentine. He believed they could be worn down, but the effect was to reduce England's first innings to a near-shambles, with the crowd twice expressing noisy disapproval, once singing in a calypso rhythm, 'We want money back.'

Walcott had made an astonishing 220 out of the West Indies' first innings total of 383, and there seemed no reason to me, with a batting line-up of Hutton, Watson, May, Compton, Graveney and the player-manager Charlie Palmer, followed by Bailey and Evans, to anticipate a failure by England.

There were three wickets down by the time I joined Hutton, and at once I felt I was in exceptional form. Ramadhin was bowling, and I cracked his first ball, a half-volley, to mid-off. The next was pitched middle and leg, and again I struck it sweetly, but unfortunately both went straight to fielders. A yard either way and I would have begun with two healthy boundaries. At the end of the over Len came down the wicket and said, 'We don't really want that. We're going to bat this one out.'

It was as if I had been placed in a strait-jacket. For the next two hours I blocked, blocked and blocked again while I squeezed fifteen runs. Eventually, almost as if it had been written into the script as an indictment and an awful warning, I was out to a boob ball – which so often happens to grim defenders. Ramadhin sent down the simplest of full-tosses on the leg side. Somehow I contrived, with a stroke best described as a lunge, to give a return catch. Ramadhin took 158 Test wickets, and I guarantee never, *never* with a worse ball.

Len slumped on his bat in disbelief, and I had better not

reveal my own thoughts at that moment, for I had been obliged to play in a way utterly foreign to me. It meant I had to stay on my back foot, locked to the crease and denied the freedom to use my reach and height. That night England's dissatisfied batsmen took up the argument with Len who, to his credit, removed the defensive shackles. As if to emphasise the folly of what had gone on before, I ran out of partners in the second innings when I was allowed to play my own game, and finished 64 not out, well satisfied with my own form but disconsolate at England's second disaster. Even so, Hutton scarcely deserved the punishment of an unfortunate decision against Denis Compton, then on 93 and going strongly, which changed the final course of the match and turned what seemed likely to be a draw into certain defeat.

Jeff Stollmeyer, the captain, cultured opening batsman and occasional spin bowler, was the stand-breaker with a googly which hit Denis on the pad about two inches outside the off stump and, in my estimation from the other end, would have bounced six inches over the top of the wicket – an opinion not exclusively my own.

While cricketers will generally accept judgements, right or wrong, as part of the game, there is a different attitude alto-gether when the issue is clear-cut and should be beyond argument. They know by instinct and judgement whether an appeal is good or bad, hairline or a try-on. A bad decision induces grumbles, for players are only human, but rank in-justice can be another matter.

One such incident in the fourth Test at Port-of-Spain brought a heap of West Indian trouble on my head and pungent criticism of English sporting standards.

In those days Trinidad had a jute mat, and the West Indies won the toss and batted. We knew we were in for a hard slog, and Stollmeyer and J.K. Holt Jnr gave them the expected solid start.

Denis Compton bowled the last over before lunch and dismissed Stollmeyer. Everton Weekes came in and, after he had pushed a single, J.K. Holt Jnr, a former Lancashire

League pro, was left to play the last ball. As Holt had never appeared to pick Compton's 'chinamen' or googlies with any assurance, I was especially alert at slip. Sure enough, Denis deceived him with a half-volley which I picked as a googly. Holt, thinking it was a 'chinaman' (the left-arm bowler's off-break to a right-handed batsman), went for a square drive and made contact with the outside edge six to eight inches up the bat. I was waiting for the catch, which could not have been more straightforward. As I always counted the number of balls in an over as part of my exercise in concentration, I began to walk to the pavilion, happy at having participated in the capture of a second wicket.

Then, to my astonishment, I heard Hutton's voice call to umpire Ellis Achong, himself a former left-arm googly bowler: 'Ellis, how's that then?' Having had probably the best view on the ground, the validity of the catch had never crossed my mind. There could be no possible doubt. I turned to see Holt still at the crease, and Compton gesticulating and saying, 'Come on, Ellis, give him out.' Achong answered, 'No, not out.'

Not at first believing the evidence of my eyes and ears, I suddenly lost my temper and threw the ball, which I still had in my hand, to the ground in disgust with the words 'That's the fourth time!' – a reference to Holt's involvement in three previous incidents in which the England players thought he had got away with it.

I was hissed and booed by the members and horribly condemned in the newspapers. In fact everyone but the English contingent had a field day. Of course I readily admit that I should have kept a stiff upper lip and all that, but I think the matter should not have been viewed in the context of one single episode. Nor am I a saint, and there has to be a breaking point for everyone. Significantly, I was not reprimanded either by captain or manager, and not one accusing word was levelled at me by the rest of the team.

By the end of the second day there was a second controversy when Everton Weekes was given not out when we in the slips and those closest to the wicket were convinced he had snicked a catch to the wicket-keeper Dick Spooner – Godfrey Evans having come out in a rash of boils. (I think he must have been sent to bed early one night!) Trevor Bailey was bowling, and his trap ball was to pitch just outside the off stump, fractionally shorter but a shade quicker. Everton, who was in cracking form, went to square cut, was late on it and got a bottom edge. Dick, able to stand up on the mat, comfortably took the catch, but the umpire, Ken Wood, refused the appeal on the grounds that though he heard a nick he did not see the ball deviate in flight. To do so in the matter of inches from bat to gloves is next to impossible, and I'll never forget the bemused look on Dick's face. 'What's going on here?' he asked.

Everton, who I always found to be a fine sportsman, can't be blamed for his luck when his score was 43. He went on to make 206, Frankie Worrell 167 and Clyde Walcott 124 and, as far as we were concerned, the three W's stood for woe, woe, woe! The West Indies scored 681 for eight declared, and England 537, and I, much to my disappointment, was out at 92.

It cannot be denied that by that stage of the tour the team were incensed by the umpiring and wearied by the depth and fervour of the criticism. It seemed as if no excuse was needed to bring out the big stick, and rumour fed on rumour.

As for umpiring around the world, I found by experience that it is necessary to develop a philosophical spirit and expect some unusual decisions. You are certainly not going to be favoured – that's for certain – and the argument against neutral umpires that all umpires are neutral is a pompous attitude which comes from an ivory tower. Before I went on my first tour to India in 1951-2, George Duckworth, the former England and Lancashire wicket-keeper, advised me: 'Don't get hit on the pad too often.'

I must have taken his words to heart because, in *Wisden*'s account of that visit to India I am complimented on enhancing my reputation (I didn't know I had one at that time!) and scoring six centuries mainly off the back foot. Clearly I wasn't going to be hit on the front pad. I suppose I was one of the very few among top batsmen who normally played almost entirely off the front foot. A possible explanation is that my method was fashioned on Bristol pitches, where there was no bounce at all. When I went to Worcester, where there was a little extra pace in the wicket, I was so entrenched in my technique that I merely played a little higher. I found I still had time to rock back and pull bouncers off the front foot, a technique not recommended in the coaching manuals.

The textbook is all very well, but I feel strongly that players, once they have acquired the basics, should develop their own strengths. We can't all be Huttons, and the more I ponder on Hutton, the batsman, and Hutton, the captain, the more I wonder at his marvellous skills, unflinching resolve and inner strengths. To come back after being two down to share the series in the West Indies in 1953–4, in the face of problem after problem and provocations enough to break the strongest will, was a staggering achievement.

For starters he was obliged to overcome an inescapable feeling that, for some reason, many in the West Indies considered it a slight to have to play host to England's first appointed professional captain. Some of the older residents were that far behind the times, and, it has to be said, there were plenty at home who saw Hutton as the symbol of a new era which they couldn't happily accept.

He had a lot to take, and I never felt more indignant on his behalf than when he was alleged to have snubbed Mr Alex Bustamante, Jamaica's extrovert Chief Minister, during the double-century innings which, along with Trevor Bailey's bowling, was to win the match and square the series. The West Indies, against all the odds, had been bowled out for 139 by Bailey, who brilliantly took advantage of a cross breeze and a little dampness in the pitch, to return figures of 7 for 34. When Hutton had come in and said he had lost the toss, our spirits had taken a down. We thought there was no way to come back. Only the day before the groundsman had cheerfully predicted a total of 700 for the side batting first.

After the stunning flop by the West Indies the scene was set for Hutton to assume charge, and he went in determined to bat for two days. We knew he had the ability and character to do exactly that, and it was fascinating to watch him take control and handle, as an example, the medium pace bowling of Denis Atkinson. Over after over was pitched on a length, and Len would play it back with studied correctness. Then, without apparent effort, he would follow through and the ball would streak to the boundary. His concentration was unbelievable, and in the end it had to be broken *off the field* by the unbelievable insensitivity of people unconnected with the game.

After nine hours Hutton went in to tea with his score at 205, and he was changing his sweat-drenched clothing when voices were raised and a stranger was heard to declare: 'This is the crowning insult.' And a lot more in a similar vein. None of us, least of all poor Len, had the remotest idea what the fuss was about, but it transpired that the Chief Minister was among the applauding members on the way to the dressing-room, and Hutton had not stopped to chat with him. A snub, an insult to the Minister, said the excitable officials, but it had to be a monumental impudence on their part to expect Hutton to talk to anyone, even an august politician, at that moment, even supposing he had been recognised.

During a big innings Hutton became completely absorbed in concentration and was impervious to all other demands. It was part of his perfect temperament. He blotted out all distractions and thought only of his batting and the ultimate objective of winning the match.

Though explanations were later accepted, and Hutton wrote a conciliatory letter to the *Daily Gleaner* and had a friendly drink with the Minister, the damage had been done. Within a few minutes of the resumption Hutton, confused and sickened by the misery of the events, played an un-Hutton-like stroke and was out without having added to his score. Those imaginative officials who had chosen to invent an insult had succeeded where the West Indies bowlers had failed, and among the team there was a mood of sympathy, tinged with indignation, for the captain. As always he had the last word – an emphatic victory which had to be a triumph of character.

When the almost daily distractions, both on and off the field, are recalled, it is nothing short of amazing that Hutton was able to maintain his own form, score 169 and 205 in the two winning Tests and finish with an average of 96.71, almost double that achieved by the next two batsmen, Compton and May. The strain he endured would have been too much for the average captain, and his critics would do well to remember his fortitude.

It is true that he made mistakes, which is the common lot of us all. It is true that he would no doubt like to expunge from the record books the Barbados (1953-4) and Brisbane (1954-5) Tests – when England lost by 181 runs and an innings and 154 respectively. Likewise the 1954 defeat by Pakistan at the Oval when an imprudent attempt was made to get the run-target of 168 to win in the 155 minutes remaining on the fourth day – with a full day to spare – and he must bear some responsibility for the tactic of slowing down over-rates. I do not accept that he started that practice, which has since plagued the game, but I agree that he took it a step or two farther on. It is true that he was often enigmatic, deep and unforthcoming, and the pressures were shown in sarcasm towards younger players. But overall, judged by the acid test of results – the winning and the retention of the Ashes was a summit achievement – his stature among the captains of England must rank high.

I also believe that much of the criticism he had to take was harsh and prejudiced, and I wonder whether, if he had been able to sail through a long career with the serenity of the older professionals, Hutton would have outstripped the batting records of Sir Jack Hobbs. In class and technique the margin between them must surely have been small to the point of insignificance. Hobbs, still regarded as the definitive genius, was never saddled with the captaincy, at least not as the appointed captain; the teams he batted in were, if we are to believe the pundits, infinitely stronger; and he had the advantage of the old lbw law.

Hutton lost six peak years to the war – Hobbs always said he was in his prime before the First World War – and returned with his left arm shorter and weaker as the result of an accident. All things considered, Hutton, I suggest, had a far rockier road than Hobbs. For one thing, how he must have yearned for an opening partner of Herbert Sutcliffe's quality to share the pressures.

I learned a lot from Len. His knowledge of the game was profound.

Like the proverbial University professor Len had his absent-minded moments. During the Lord's Test in the Coronation year of 1953 the players were presented to the Queen. The teams were lined up in front of the pavilion, and Len's task as captain was formally to introduce each England player. When my turn came he looked at me as if he was surprised to see me there.

'This is . . . er . . .' he began, and his voice trailed away. Her Majesty smiled, shook hands and passed on.

A year later, at Trinidad, Len introduced me to the then Archbishop of York as 'Tom Goddard'. Goddard, of course, was my Gloucestershire team-mate who, when told of the incident, said, 'Well, that's all right, as long as I'm not introduced as Tom Graveney!'

Still, I suppose it was an improvement on 'Mr Gravity'.

Probably because I got on so famously with him I enjoyed the captaincy of Colin Cowdrey most of all – though it's a difficult choice to make. Maybe in a cricket sense we were kindred spirits in our outlook. Colin preferred the touch of quiet persuasion, and fretted if his standards could not be maintained. They said he lacked the killer touch and held back, but the fact is, when he held the captaincy without looking over his shoulders, as in the West Indies in 1967–8, precious little justified criticism could be mounted against him. *Wisden* went so far as to declare that no other captain could have led the side so well and 'performed the numerous duties of captaincy so flawlessly in the exacting circumstances of the tour.'

The curious background to his appointment had been that the Board of Control's selectors had wanted Brian Close as tour leader – the MCC Committee overruled them after he was accused of deliberate delaying tactics when captaining Yorkshire in a county match at Edgbaston – and that decision coincided with the retirement of Mike Smith. That chain of events virtually made Cowdrey the third choice. As I became vice-captain when Freddie Titmus had the boating accident, which cost him four toes, I was very close to Cowdrey and can vouch for everything said in his praise. Without being subjected to the same problems Hutton had to endure, he had his mettle tested by what *Wisden* later described as sub-standard umpiring and unruly crowds. A riot at Sabina Park, which turned probable victory into near defeat, was enough for one tour, but he had also been booed in Trinidad, where he played two magnificent innings, and in Guyana he had to wait at the ground before he could be escorted to the team's hotel. No unbiased judge could possibly fail to put Cowdrey ahead of Sir Gary Sobers in all the accepted arts of captaincy in that series.

Nothing seemed more certain than that Cowdrey would achieve his life-long ambition to take England to Australia in 1970–71, the ultimate aim for any English cricketer, but, after he injured the Achilles tendon in his left foot, Ray Illingworth, whose name had not been on any lips, came from nowhere to leave both Cowdrey and me in the cold. Colin was devastatingly unlucky. I am never sure, for instance, why Brian Close took over from him in the fifth Test in 1966. Perhaps Cowdrey did not push himself enough. He should have been the natural successor to Peter May, but something went wrong. In 1966, when I came back after three years on the shelf, England had three captains: first Mike Smith, then Cowdrey, and finally Close at The Oval. The difference between them was that Smith lost his one match by an innings, Cowdrey had two defeats and a draw, while Close won by an innings and 32 runs – Eureka, cried English cricket, a captain has been found to beat the unbeatable West Indies.

There was no doubt about it being a stirring occasion, but Brian didn't half have some luck. England's last three wickets produced a record 361 runs. Seven wickets were down for 166 in reply to the West Indies' 268 when John Murray and I put on 217 for the eighth wicket, which is still a record for England against the West Indies, and John Snow and Ken Higgs added 128 for the last wicket. Between them the last three, Murray (112), Higgs (63) and Snow (59 not out), aggregated 234, only 34 less than the West Indies first innings and nine more than Conrad Hunte, Rohan Kanhai, Basil Butcher, Seymour Nurse, Sobers and the rest managed in the second.

Yet only Murray and I know how England's rescue operation hung on the thread of a brilliant decision by the late Syd Buller, who must have been the best umpire of all time. I cannot believe that Frank Chester could have improved on Syd's amazing ability to be 99 per cent right. I had seen Dennis Amiss, Basil D'Oliveira, Brian Close and Ray Illingworth come and go when Murray, playing back first ball to Charlie Griffith, was hit on the pads smack in front of the wicket. Charlie went up, Jackie Hendricks, the wicket-keeper, went up, and from where I stood as the non-striker there was no question about the verdict. The noise from the West Indian supporters was virtually non-stop, which made umpiring all the more difficult. Buller, however, firmly denied the appeal, and at the end of the over Murray said it had been the right decision. 'I got an edge all right,' he said, 'but with all this noise I couldn't have complained if I'd gone.'

Close consolidated his position with public approval and victories over India and Pakistan in the following split-tour summer, but he came an awful cropper through what might

A little practice with my son Tim on the day I was selected for England in 1966.

My three best friends – Becky, Tim and Jackie.

With my brother Ken, one of the select few bowlers to have taken ten wickets in an innings.

The favourite shot – this one went for four.

Magnificent colleagues: Godfrey Evans bags another victim, Dave Fletcher of Surrey, with Trevor Bailey at slip.

Ray Lindwall. The greatest of them all?

'Gravity' meets Royalty. Colin Cowdrey and Ken Barrington look on as I shake hands with HM the Queen at Lord's in 1968.

I reach my century at Queen's Park, Trinidad, in 1968 with an off-drive off Wes Hall (on the ground).

The great Len Hutton (*left*), opening the innings
for England with Don Kenyon, my captain at
Worcestershire.

With my great friend and colleague Basil D'Oliveira and Sir George Dowty, the
industrialist, who was instrumental in bringing me to Worcestershire.

The explosive face of West Indian cricket. *Left*: Clyde Walcott. *Right*: Everton Weekes. *Below*: The riot at Sabina Park, Jamaica, in 1968. As the tear-gas drifts into the pavilion, Colin Cowdrey and I walk off the field with Les Ames, followed by Gary Sobers and David Holford.

Wes Hall bowls, Graveney backs up. West Indies
versus the Duke of Norfolk's XI, Arundel 1966.

Gary Sobers, master with both bat and ball.

Unexpected partnerships. *Above*: Opening the innings for England with Fred Trueman at Bombay, where I made a century in each innings. Neither of us had been selected for the 1956–57 South African tour. *Below*: Perched above Edgbaston with Peter West, a supremely professional colleague in my new career as a television commentator.

be termed his own stubborness. How often a cricketer's very strengths become an achilles heel! Charged with deliberate time-wasting at Edgbaston – nowadays a minimum of twenty overs have to be bowled in the last hour – Close would not back down or apologise. Had he done so he would have continued as captain.

A strange story, but truth to tell, I found Close's captaincy a shade odd. I freely acknowledge his bravery and success at Yorkshire – four championships in seven years and a Gillette Cup – but in the field you would eventually find yourself covering every blade of grass on the ground. He gave me the impression he was shifting his field around for the benefit of the press box and to make certain the spectators had no doubt who was in charge. Brian was tough all right, mighty tough and unyielding, and crowds rightly love a fighter. By sheer force of personality and a commendable belligerence he made his presence felt but, tactically, he was not as good as his reputation – certainly he could not measure up to Ray Illingworth, who knew exactly what he was doing. Like Hutton Ray set himself long-term objectives. He has a fine cricket brain.

My one Test under Freddie Brown, who did so much to lift England off the floor in the team-building years after the war, was that rather rum occasion against South Africa at Old Trafford in 1951. I doubt whether it was a standard performance, as Brown, a commanding figure with an undoubted presence, had a reputation among players as a bit of a martinet. Some of the Northamptonshire team were rather intimidated by his forthright approach, and yet he could be one of the boys. They knew him as 'The Boss' but, again, he did make something of a county which was more familiar with failure than success.

Without in any sense being priggish, Brown was one of the old school of no-nonsense captains, who rightly were very conscious of the need to maintain traditional standards of behaviour on the field. He was firm but fair, and he would have given some of today's petulant extroverts short shrift.

They would have had to behave, or get booted out. Sadly, there are no Freddie Browns to bring sanity to modern cricket. If there were, the game could be cleaned up in a season.

I was grateful for some advice he gave to me early in my career with Gloucestershire. We were playing in Northamptonshire and part of the crowd gave me verbal stick when I was put on to bowl – successfully, as it turned out. My callow reaction was to give a V-sign. After the match Freddie, the opposing captain, sought me out, congratulating me on my performance, and, in a fatherly way, told me never to express my feelings in that way again.

Players today tell me they are more 'emotionally involved' than in my time. Tripe, of course. The words are 'less disciplined'.

Ted Dexter seemed, like Cowdrey, a gift to the establishment. His background was right; he was a glorious striker of the ball; an elegant stroke-maker; a veritable throw-back to the Corinthian age. When it came down to it, Ted had too many conflicting interests to have the single-minded purposefulness of a Test captain. He loved the horses, dabbled with politics (actually contesting the seat held by James Callaghan), had business connections in closed-circuit television, and, just to emphasise his versatility, he piloted his family in his own light aircraft to Australia when he became a newspaper correspondent.

County cricket, I fear, was too humdrum and demanded too much discipline for a man with his free-ranging ideas, and for England I never knew what to expect from him. He was too much of a theorist. One of his ideas, nourished by Alan Davidson, was that leg-spinners were the bowlers to fiddle wickets on good pitches. Fine, if leg-spinners are available. Ted looked around his team in Australia in 1962–3 and his eye alighted on Ken Barrington and me. Barrington, yes; Graveney, emphatically no! Ken had started at The Oval as a leg-break bowler and was a very useful support in Australia, but to be accurate it is necessary to have a lot of bowling. For two or three overs it is possible to bowl respectably, but it is hard to continue dropping on a length. The talent to invite my envy belonged to Bob Barber, but he seemed disinclined to use it, though he could spin and make the ball bounce. He could have been another Benaud, and I am sure few would dispute the contention that Bob was a better batsman.

Peter May was another of my England skippers. Having learned the job from Hutton, he played it hard and tight and became stereotyped in his tactics and methods. He had a ghastly time at the height of the throwing controversy and, in this respect, can be classed as desperately unlucky. Peter was much liked and respected, and it was a pity that his captaincy did not measure up to his towering ability as a batsman.

9
Typhoon in the Islands

One of the major resentments of Hutton's tourists in the Caribbean stemmed from the uncontrolled rumours and distortions of fact which followed the team from island to island like a bad odour. Gossip fed on gossip and waxed fat. As soon as one story died, there was another to take its place. Individuals were blamed, notably the voluble Freddie Trueman and Tony Lock, for alleged misdeeds which were nothing more than figments of mischievous imaginations. Too often, it seemed, people wanted to believe the worst, and I found myself in deep trouble defending the reputations of Denis Compton, Godfrey Evans and Trevor Bailey who – like Trueman – were deservedly popular among the ordinary cricket followers.

At a reception at the Barbados Yacht Club after the Bridgetown Test, I listened to some rubbish from an official from Jamaica who, I afterwards learned, stayed at Government House. Eventually I took exception to a remark he made about Compton, Evans and Bailey, and, as he appeared to give himself the freedom to say what he liked, I thought I should at least have the same privilege. Another time I would have merely turned my back on him. But I was depressed after the defeat, tired of hearing my friends and team-mates being criticised, and it was after midnight.

The following morning I was first down to breakfast – my habit, as on tour I liked to follow a routine – and was idly watching the cheeky sparrows coming in and stealing sugar from the tables when Penny Robins arrived. Penny, the daughter of the former England and Middlesex captain Walter Robins, was acting as secretary to Charlie Palmer, the player-manager.

'What were you doing last night?' she asked.

'Why, nothing much. I had a reasonable night considering we lost the Test,' I replied.

'Well,' said Penny, 'Len and Charlie are at Government House discussing whether or not you are to be sent home.'

My first reaction was that it was too early in the morning to have one's leg pulled, but apparently it had been reported that I had insulted a guest at the Yacht Club.

'You're joking,' I said in genuine amazement. 'I'd never have thought it important enough to have given it a second thought.'

Yet there it was, clear evidence of the paper-thin ice on which the MCC skated. Cables were flying between Barbados and Lord's as the authorities debated whether I was to continue the tour, or be sent back to England on disciplinary grounds. Clearly I had two doughty champions in the captain and manager, who had enough on their minds without having to deal with petty molehills turned into Everests, and I heard nothing more. The management put it into perspective and left it at that. Lord Cornwallis was MCC President at the time, and who should I find in the chair when I entered the committee room at Lord's seeking registration with Worcestershire after my departure from Gloucestershire ... yes, none other than Lord Cornwallis.

In view of my misadventures in Trinidad and Barbados, I was agreeably surprised to be invited to join E.W. Swanton's goodwill, bridge-building tour in March and April 1956, even though I only came in to fill a vacancy. Jim, who knows a thing or two, restricted his tour to Barbados and Trinidad. Originally he had invited South Africans, including Roy McLean and Johnny Waite, but the West Indies refused to have them, and I joined a team captained by Colin Cowdrey and including Colin Ingleby-Mackenzie, Hubert Doggart, a recent President of MCC, Johnny Warr, Robin Marlar, Frank Tyson, Gamini Goonesena, Alan Oakman and Micky Stewart.

With tensions eased – I wondered how much the publicity given to the West Indies' claim to be World Champions contributed to Hutton's problems – I enjoyed myself immensely as I took 154 off Barbados and 117 off Trinidad. Immediately after the match against a West Indies XI at Port-of-Spain, Stewart dashed home to play for Corinthian Casuals in a replayed FA Amateur Cup final with Bishop Auckland, but bad weather delayed his plane and he arrived at Middlesbrough five minutes after the match had started.

Tyson still had spells when he was unbelievably fast, and his confrontations with Clyde Walcott and Everton Weekes were classics deserving a bigger stage than a private tour. That winter the West Indies had toured New Zealand. Walcott had not gone, but Weekes had started with five successive centuries and ended with six out of ten innings. He could be said to have been in form.

In our first match at Bridgetown, Walcott had made two when he was beaten by a yorker which sent his stumps disappearing in all directions. He had barely started to pick his bat up. That was his only innings of the match. In the next game, again against Barbados, Walcott was again yorked, this time third ball for nought. In the second innings Tyson was less fresh, and it was fascinating to see Walcott adopt a new technique – a great batsman's thinking reaction to a problem. Instead of his normal pick-up, which included a hint of 'wind', he merely pushed from the blockhole – far less elegant but highly effective, for he went on to conquer Frank and score 130.

Weekes played for the West Indies XI and shortly after he came in Frank let him have a bouncer. He went to hook it, but it was on to him so quickly that it hit the top edge and flew almost directly over the wicket-keeper's head. Everton turned to me in the slips and said, 'He's too fast to hook.'

There had been a measure of suspicion that the famous W's were as vulnerable to the bumper and really quick bowling as the rest of the international batsmen of the time. They failed against Ray Lindwall and Keith Miller in the 1951-2 series in Australia, when Worrell averaged 33.70, Weekes 24.50 and Walcott 14.50. Weekes was badly handicapped then by a thigh muscle injury, and, as counter-evidence, there was his remarkable 90 on a spiteful pitch at Lord's in 1957. From slip I marvelled at his skill in dealing with the nasty risers from Freddie Trueman, Brian Statham and Trevor Bailey, and at his bravery, for he broke a finger and was constantly hit on the body and arms.

As far as I am concerned there can be no sensible argument about the status of the W's, but if it can be said that there was a chink in their armour – and all things are relative – it could have been against authentic fast bowling, with the proviso that it needed to be very fast and very good. To an extent they did not have an abundance of practice against top-class bowlers in the West Indies at the time. Apart from Hines Johnson and Frank King for a few overs, there was little in the way of speed; certainly nothing to compare in quality and numbers with the current crop.

Also I felt the openers Jeff Stollmeyer and the left-handed Allan Rae were not given the credit they were due. By the time they had taken the edge off the bowling, the killers were ready to tear it apart. Stollmeyer, tall and upstanding, and Rae were a very fine opening pair. Rae himself would not have pretended to be a stylist, but, my goodness, he did everything asked of him and a lot more.

Watching 'Typhoon' Tyson attack Walcott and Weekes confirmed my conviction, formed in Australia in 1954-5, that at his peak he must rank as the fastest bowler of all time. I cannot believe any bowler could be faster than he was during the Sydney Test, a view endorsed by Sir Don Bradman to me. There was a stiff wind down pitch from the Hill end, and he was terrifying. At first slip I was fifty yards back and closer to the pickets in front of the pavilion than I was to the bat. In fact there was no logically correct position to stand because if there was a snick – and I admit to a secret prayer that one would not come to me – it followed no conventional path and went like a tracer bullet. I was interested to hear Bob Wyatt telling a similar story during the Melbourne centenary Test of the time he fielded at slip to Harold Larwood in similar conditions at Sydney.

Looking back it is fascinating to reflect on the little incidents which help to shape destiny. After the first disaster at Brisbane, when Tyson's only wicket, that of Richie Benaud, cost him 160 runs, the prospect of him becoming a victorious spearhead and a legend would have been dismissed as a fantasy. Yet before the second Test, helped by Alf Gover, former England and Surrey bowler and a notable coach, who by chance was in Australia, Tyson overhauled his technique. One valuable change was to cut down his run-up. Alec Bedser, still suffering the after-effects of an attack of shingles, was only half fit, but Tyson might not even have held his place but for a significant spell against Neil Harvey in the match with Victoria a week before Sydney.

Tyson's improvement was so marked that he took 6 for 68 in Victoria's first innings, but Hutton, still grimly determined on his policy of speed, was more interested in Harvey's failure to land a bat on him at one period than in his overall figures, impressive though they were. In the midst of Harvey's embarrassment as he played and missed, a stentorian voice roared, 'Bowl 'im a piannah – he might be able to play that.'

No doubt Tyson was much helped by the pitches, which fell a long way short of the expectations of the batsmen, but in so many instances he showed that he had a cricket brain as well as exceptional brawn. No longer was Keith Miller able to square-cut him as he had done with such savage strength at Brisbane, and not only was his length better, but there was evidence of a thinking bowler.

Batting before lunch on the fourth day Tyson was felled by a fearsome blow on the back of the head when he turned his back on a bumper from Lindwall. I remember to this day the chill of apprehension which passed through the England dressing-room, but, being as tough as they come, he not only recovered but bowled Australia out the next day. Ray was among those who expected a retaliatory bumper when he batted, but Tyson immediately yorked him, as he did Jimmy Burke and Graeme Hole.

The combination of Tyson's speed and Statham's accuracy was irresistible. While I had my successes against Freddie Trueman, Statham, whose action seemed to make the ball skid through, was wont to roll me over far too often for my liking.

Tyson's triumphs inevitably had a short life. The strongest human frame could not have stood the wear and tear of bowling at his speed, and he did not get much help from the Northampton pitches, which were more suited to the needs of their Australian spinners, George Tribe and Jack Manning.

Frank often bowled a few overs with the new ball and was then unemployed for the rest of the innings unless a big partnership developed. Once Frank, bowling to me in the nets in Australia, hit me in the ribs with such force that I was put out of a state game – and he was bowling off three paces!

My main regret was not having the opportunity to play against Ray Lindwall in 1948, though I was to see enough of him in later years. Yet, as twelfth man for Gloucestershire, I had a fleeting glimpse into Australian methods which remained etched on my mind throughout my career. One of my duties was to tell the opposition's batsmen, Arthur Morris and Syd Barnes, that Gloucestershire were taking the field. As the batsmen left, Lindsay Hassett, the acting captain, called out, 'This fellow Goddard . . . we don't want him.'

Tom Goddard, then approaching fifty, was still one of the most devastating off-spinners in the country, having taken over 200 wickets the previous year. His partnership with Sam Cook, the left-arm spinner, was a match-winner, and Hassett sensed danger both in the current match and possibly in a future Test in the series. The Aussies planned to remove him

from contention, and it was accomplished in the most spectacular fashion. As soon as Tom came on and his arm neared
the top before the moment of delivering the ball, they danced
down the pitch to meet him. The idea of playing his spin
from the crease, hemmed in by a circle of close catchers,
never occurred to them. Morris was dazzling, scoring a century before lunch, another between lunch and tea, and 290 in
all with a six and forty-two fours. The Australians made 774
for 7 declared and Goddard conceded 186 in 32 overs without
taking a wicket – one of five bowlers with 100 runs or more,
considerably more in fact, against them.

   I never saw a more clinically efficient job on a cricket field,
and against a bowler who had so much talent and experience.
Goddard could spin the ball even on lifeless wickets, and he
had natural flight. He never knew why; it just happened. The
ball used to slide out. When sand was put in thousands of
fork marks in the Bristol pitch in 1947, Goddard and Cook
were too much for county opposition and almost won the
championship. Without sand it was slow and bounceless. But
the way Morris and the Aussies handled Goddard served as
a lasting lesson to me, and it was one potent reason why it
went so much against the grain to be ordered to play Sonny
Ramadhin, who was so difficult to pick – indeed the best
method was to treat him as an off-spinner – and Alf Valentine
from the crease.

10
Quickies and Chuckers

Leeds, 1966, was the most unpleasant of my seventy-nine Tests. To have to condemn it as a lousy game of cricket is particulary sad as the West Indies, with Australian scalps already under their belt, confirmed their status as World Champions by taking the rubber. And the towering genius of their captain Sir Gary Sobers was given free rein with a top score of 174 and eight wickets for 80 runs. Showing skills to take the breath away, he scored a hundred between lunch and tea and became the first to reach 5,000 Test runs and 100 wickets. Poor Seymour Nurse's achievement in scoring his first century off England was overshadowed, yet he played his full part in reducing some very fine bowlers like John Snow, Ken Higgs, Basil D'Oliveira, Fred Titmus and Derek Underwood to near-impotency.

The atmosphere began to crackle with tension when England batted and the redoubtable Charlie Griffith, the man mountain with an action to cause raging controversy, was cautioned for throwing by Charlie Elliot. I can write feelingly about what was freely described at the time as a 'vicious bouncer', as I was at the receiving end. Colin Milburn had retired after being hit on his left elbow when he did not offer a stroke to Wes Hall, bowling down the slope at a terrifying pace.

England were 18 for 2 when I took my first ball from Charlie at the football end. I saw his huge frame lumbering up, but I did not see the ball until it was two yards away and going straight for my head. Sheer instinct and self preservation prompted me to get out of the way, and I felt the ball brush the back of my neck. If it had hit me I might not have been writing these words. As I straightened up and collected my wits I saw Elliott walk from square-leg walk to his colleague Syd Buller, and later he confirmed that it was, in his opinion, an illegal delivery.

After the two umpires had conferred, they agreed that Elliott should caution Griffith. Buller said, 'You have got to do it now if you're going to.' Elliott turned to Griffith and warned him: 'You can bowl, Charlie, but any more like that and I will have to call you. That delivery to Graveney was illegal.'

I couldn't have agreed more!

A lot of the fire and passion went out of Griffith's attack, and his reduced pace produced only one more wicket in the two England innings – and that only when Basil D'Oliveira, having been in an upsetting incident with Sobers, lost his cool and skied a ball to cover after scoring 88. When Dolly was 65 and doing his best to hold the fort with seven wickets down he tried to hit Lance Gibbs over mid-wicket where Conrad Hunte was the solitary fielder – I think Dolly was a bit affronted at such a field placing on a batting surface that was still good.

Dolly didn't quite middle the ball, which went straight in the direction of Hunte but began to dip. Hunte, the evangelist who gave his tour earnings to the cause of Moral Re-armament, dived forward and held the ball up in triumphant declaration of a catch. No one for an instant believed that Conrad was making a false claim, but the fielder is not always infallibly right – and one classic case occurred when Colin Cowdrey was given out in a Test at Brisbane. Dolly, who is equally straight and honest, was also certain there was a doubt and Conrad might have taken it on the half-volley. So he stood his ground.

The West Indies fieldsmen told Basil to walk, and Sobers

came up and said, 'Conrad never cheats.' Dolly replied, 'Maybe, but he didn't catch it.' When Charlie Elliott refused to uphold the appeal, there was a bitter and heated exchange between D'Oliveira and Sobers, who had known each other from League days.

What upset Dolly more than anything else was the apparent grudge held by the West Indies fielders, who made their feelings totally clear when they did not clap him off the field. To be accurate, ten of the team withheld their applause. By a splendid irony – reflecting the character of the man himself – the exception was Conrad Hunte. Dolly felt that, despite the hasty words in the heat of the moment, all should have been forgotten once the umpire's decision had been given. Knowing Basil as I do, I am sure that if it had gone against him he would have accepted it even if he had privately felt he had been wronged. The rift was not healed until the post-match drinks – and, by then, there had been another regrettable incident.

Colin Cowdrey went into the victors' dressing-room to offer his congratulations and was abruptly rebuffed without either captain or manager intervening. Sadly Colin went to his car (number plate MCC 307 – his highest score) to see one side scarred by coins from bumper to bumper. After that, an innings defeat, and the dressing-room brush-off, I doubt if Colin was too badly upset to be one of six dropped for The Oval Test, and to pass the captaincy over to Brian Close. Despite two failures in the Leeds game I held my place and scored 165. The good fortune of the selectors at The Oval was that John Snow (59 not out) – one of the six, but recalled when John Price dropped out – took part in a dramatic last-wicket stand of 128 with Ken Higgs (63). Neither had previously scored a fifty in first-class cricket.

Charlie Griffith might have been excused the belief that the devil himself was clamped to his shoulder in the mid-sixties, when his action was constantly under criticism and scrutiny. Before the 1966 visit to England, Richie Benaud, armed with camera, was the most candid of critics in the West

Indies – Australia series, and at the end of that tour some articles under Norman O'Neill's name provoked an official protest from the President of the West Indies Board of Control. It did not pass unnoticed that Richie had been Australia's captain in the acrimonious rubber when Ian Meckiff, Keith Slater, Gordon Rorke and Jimmy Burke, all regarded as suspect, helped to overthrow (if that be the right word!) Peter May's side.

Richie's swift reply would be that he captained, not selected, his Australia side, but the fact remains the West Indies ignored the mounting criticism of Griffith's action. Nevertheless Charlie himself must have been under considerable strain, and matters were not helped by his being called for throwing by the late Arthur Fagg in the match against Lancashire at Old Trafford, and nine times for overstepping the crease in the third Test at Trent Bridge.

Both Syd Buller, who must have been the best umpire of all time, and Charlie Elliott clearly gave his action the closest examination, sometimes crossing from square-leg to point to do so. Griffith, who must have been acutely conscious of what was going on, kept himself in check until the end, when he unleashed a bumper which hit Derek Underwood, England's Number 11, in the mouth. As his side were coasting to victory, I can't think what made Charlie do it. He had bowled several during the match – one just missed Cowdrey's head – but it is one thing bowling a bumper to a recognised batsman, and quite another when the batsman is not technically equipped to defend himself. If he could do so, he wouldn't be last man in. We in the dressing-room were less than impressed and, at Sobers' insistence, Charlie wrote an apology to the victim. Earlier Ray Illingworth, who devised a good technique against the quicks, was so surprised by the sudden change of pace from one of Charlie's bouncers that he was caught off his glove, which he had instinctively put up to shield his face.

Griffith, I suspect, did not enjoy his Test cricket, and much the same could be said of many of his opposing batsmen, who, like myself, saw the ball come from behind his ear, not knowing whether to prepare for a bumper to leap dementedly at the head or a swinging yorker to creep under the bat. Incidentally it would have been most instructive to have seen the upright stance favoured by Tony Greig and Mike Brearley, among others, against Griffith's yorker.

Top batsmen pick up the line and to some degree the pace from the bowler's arm as it rotates from a three o'clock position to twelve o'clock, the moment at which the ball is released. The action of the chucker often makes that well-nigh impossible, but at the same time he is often so wildly inaccurate that the side needs a leaping goalkeeper rather than a wicket-keeper to stop the widely sprayed deliveries. The amazing feature of Griffith was his accuracy, which had to be a powerful point in his favour. When I first saw him at Worcester in 1963 he had not yet drawn large-scale criticism on his head – and it has to be said it mostly came from former Test players – and I was flabbergasted that first-class cricketers could not pick him up. As I managed 75 out of a first innings total of 119, I saw plenty of him and he was absolutely spot on.

Chuckers come in two main classes. There is the thrower who has a permanently bent arm, and there is the normally legitimate bowler who slips in the occasional throw when tired or striving to bowl beyond his natural pace. A third type is the crafty operator who consciously slips in a throw to deceive an unsuspecting batsman. The chances of an umpire spotting an occasional throw are far smaller than if he is looking for it, and I, along with the other batsmen of my time, could name bowlers who got away with the doubtful ploy for years in county cricket.

Big Charlie soaked up the criticism like a sponge – or ignored it – and was inclined to blame his opponents for bleating. I, for one, thought it prudent to maintain a discreet silence, though I never had any doubt that the blame for the mess the game got itself into should be laid squarely at the door of the authorities. The various Boards were pitifully weak in passing the buck on to the umpires, some of whom argued, in turn, that bowlers would not be chosen for Test matches in the first place if they were throwers. So a shameful situation was allowed to build up.

Perhaps because he was so conscientious and always tried like mad for England, Kenny Barrington made his views public by withdrawing from a match in which Griffith was playing. While I sympathised, I thought this was a tactical mistake as it had the effect of drawing attention to his aversion to the bumper and the suspect bowler. The effect was to draw the enemy fire, so to speak, and thereafter, whenever he played against Griffith, the cry of 'Put Charlie on' went up as Ken walked to the wicket. Despite all the pressure, it has to be said that Ken never showed his feelings or flinched from physical danger – and, believe me, batsmen in the middle sixties often felt they were at the wrong end of a coconut shy on bad pitches.

Griffith and Wes Hall, another magnificent figure, were a terrifying pair. Wes was so strong that he could shift a sight-screen when he put his massive shoulder to it, and his spells of endurance, with his flannels and shirt as wet from sweat as if he had dived into a river, are legendary. Twice in 1963 he snapped middle stumps as if they were fragile pieces of balsa wood. Had I been granted a choice I doubt if I would have selected Wes to bowl the first ball to me in my comeback innings at Lord's in 1966.

I never had a more testing moment, both emotionally and as a player embarking on a career on his thirty-ninth birthday. The fact that the selectors had put their trust in me was heartening, albeit a responsibility, but I was totally unprepared for the nostalgia of the occasion and the public's warmth. To my astonishment the clapping started as I walked through the Long Room and was taken up by the crowd and accompanied me all the way to the wicket. My immediate reaction was to ask myself, 'What the heck's going on? It's only me, Tom Graveney – not Bradman, Hutton, Compton or May!' Then I sensed being part of that immense throng surrounding me; part, even perhaps a symbol, of the vast freemasonry of cricket lovers; humbly small and very, very surprised.

I might well have been engulfed by sentiment, a victim of affectionate generosity, but for one significant little act which rescued me from the clouds, and triggered a warning in my brain. I noticed Seymour Nurse dash from his position at slip at the pavilion end to Wes Hall, who was standing waiting by his bowling mark away down at the Nursery sightscreen (or so it seemed).

As Seymour and I had been together on unofficial tours, I knew exactly what advice was being passed – to let me have a short pitcher, as I always liked to get on to my front foot early in an innings. Sure enough it came, but I still went forward and gave myself time to rock back and deal with the ball.

Important though that innings was to me, I did not consciously concentrate more than in any other innings. I always felt, like Denis Compton, that it is better to play normally and not gird the loins, so to speak, in unnatural effort. In fact the only time I knew I was concentrating harder was when I was not playing well, and it could have been argued that I was not playing well *because* I was trying and concentrating too hard.

At Lord's on that very special day for me I felt relaxed and well pleased with my first sixty runs, but the trial I had undergone seemed to catch up with me and, unwisely cutting at a rising ball from Hall, I was caught at the wicket four short of a century. Everyone commiserated, but, much as I would have enjoyed a century, a score of 96 was not to be sneezed at. I suppose it was natural enough for me to remember that innings and to forget the second half of the match, when there was the real threat of Hall and Griffith turning the Test upside down. Having collected a badly bruised thumb I was not intended to bat again except in an emergency. But when Hall dismissed Colin Cowdrey and Jim Parks with successive deliveries, the red light began to show and I was sent in with the immediate task of preventing a hat-trick – with one effective hand.

Somehow I held on while Colin Milburn released the genius of his aggression, and we were still not parted after 110 minutes with 130 added, which, incredible to relate, remains a fifth wicket record by England against the West Indies. Colin made 126 to my 30. I felt singularly privileged to watch from twenty-two yards the refined savagery of his strokes. I wondered how far he would go in the game, with his gift for selecting the balls to hit and his experience growing. There seemed no limits. Had I been able to look into the future to see the fate which was to befall him, I think I would have shed tears.

There is little doubt in my mind that England's batting strength never fully recovered from the losses sustained by the almost simultaneous departure of Colin Milburn, Ken Barrington and Colin Cowdrey, through accident, illness and injury; Ted Dexter's retirement and my ban, followed by Geoff Boycott's decision to go into voluntary personal liquidation for three years.

Losing established run-getters was only one aspect of the problem, for it is absolutely essential for the new and untried batsmen to have the benefit of able and experienced players around them when they make the considerable leap from county to international cricket. To my mind the gap is ever-widening. That was where Neil Harvey, marginally better than Greg Chappell as Australia's finest post-war batsman, scored so heavily.

When he was introduced at Test level, he followed Don Bradman, Arthur Morris, Syd Barnes and Lindsay Hassett in the Australian order. Of course he was so good that he would have succeeded in any company, but the fact that he was cushioned by genuine class on all sides must have helped his confidence and speeded his progress. Nowadays all too often the newcomer has to shoulder an awesome burden and knows he cannot afford to fail.

Reverting to the subject of throwing, I could never understand why it took so long as it did for the powers that be to decide that Ian Meckiff and South Africa's Geoff Griffin had bent arms at some point in their actions. Positive action from the start could have saved no end of trouble and spared two nice blokes much bitter controversy. The mistake England made over Meckiff was not to make an official complaint right away as Godfrey Evans advocated. I was one of the players who lined the dressing-room windows to watch Meckiff loosening up in front of the pavilion at Melbourne before MCC's match with Victoria. Ian was bowling at half-pace, and it was all too obvious that the advanced whispers reaching us about his action were justified. 'Now's the time to do something about it,' urged Godfrey, but the general opinion seemed to be wait and see.

Ian took five wickets in the match, but seemed so inaccurate that most of the team didn't think it worth making a fuss over – a double error, because a thrower is a thrower whether he's good at it or not. Also it meant facing the later charge of squealing only after Meckiff started to bowl straighter and had taken nine wickets, including 6 for 38 in the second Test at Melbourne. And once a row starts, Australia's instinctive reaction is to stand four square and defend their position at all costs, with opinions pitched in from people clearly not understanding the first thing about cricket, let alone the technicalities of bowling actions.

As always there were exceptions, with Ray Lindwall and Alan Davidson apt to express their opinions with Red Indian-style war cries and the claim to be the last of the straight-arm bowlers. At the time their tribe seemed to be in danger of extinction! I do, however, give Australia full credit for the way they finally grasped the nettle, though most of Peter May's side would have preferred action before and not after the tour.

Tony Lock also came out of the controversy well and was to be commended for the determined way he went about remodelling his style. His faster ball was the very devil to spot, and when I say fast I mean fast. George Headley, the 'black

Bradman' who was unwisely plucked from the semi-retirement of the Birmingham League by public subscription in his native Jamaica, to play in the 1954 Test at Sabina Park, was a victim of Tony's faster ball. I doubt if the victim was alone in not picking up the delivery. Lock was later no-balled for throwing, and again at Barbados – three times in one day – and for the rest of the tour wisely cut out his faster ball.

A lot of us in county cricket thought both Tony and Peter Loader were guilty of the occasional throw, which did not diminish my respect for their huge ability. The story goes that Doug Insole, on being bowled by Lock, blandly asked the umpire if he had been bowled or run out!

South Africa's decision to send Griffin to England in 1960 flew in the face of common sense. Perhaps, unlike the rest of us, they saw nothing wrong in his action, and they had the encouragement of history. No visiting bowler in England at that time had ever been no-balled for throwing, and it is common 'inside' knowledge that Frank Chester was forbidden to take action against the South African fast bowler Cuan McCarthy during the 1951 tour. *Wisden* prudently observed: 'Not for the first time South Africa gambled on a fast bowler with a doubtful action. In 1951 McCarthy escaped official disapproval on the part of the umpires.'

Unfortunately for Griffin – the one I felt sorry for – there was a new and alarmed attitude a decade later, and, despite the clear warnings of being no-balled for throwing in the MCC match at Lord's and again at Trent Bridge and Southampton, he was pitched into the second Test at Lord's. Moreover there was an obvious plan to 'hide' him from Syd Buller at square-leg. Nevertheless Frank Lee no-balled him eleven times for throwing. As the Test finished early, an exhibition game was put on which brought the issue to the boil. This time Buller, put to the test, no-balled Griffin four times in five deliveries and the over was completed under-arm. The guilty men were those who exposed Griffin to such an ordeal. To the fury of players and public alike, Buller did not umpire again in the series, following a South African objection.

Frank Lee, who had been even more involved, rightly carried on, but Buller, conscientious to a degree and, in my opinion, the Number 1 umpire of all time, was penalised for doing what he felt was right. The fee he would have received for umpiring a later Test in the series was paid to him, but cricket was much the poorer for betraying one of its sacred principles. As *Wisden* wrote: 'Umpires have a difficult time already, and when they are told to hold laws in abeyance, no one should be surprised if they take the easy way out and let things slide.'

Cricket has cause to look back on Buller's treatment on this occasion with embarrassment, and the county captains in the December of that year went out of their way to nominate him for the umpires' Test panel for the visit of Australia in the following season.

I recall the dressing-room discussions over Sonny Ramadhin - not only about the best way to play the perplexing little spinner, but whether his bowling absolutely conformed to the law. Some suggested he was a 'little' thrower, a description which is easier for the cricketer to understand than it is to explain in print. The position from which he delivered the ball aroused severe suspicion, and he always had his sleeves down and buttoned at the wrists, which made his movement difficult to scrutinise. I also remember him releasing a bumper and a beamer at Peter May in a Trinidad Test - something of a feat for a spinner.

Sonny was an original, and very difficult to spot. His stock ball came in from the off, and on to the bat with surprising speed, and was varied by the ball going the other way or straightening out. With his quick arm action and a flick of the wrist he was anything but easy to pick, and Clyde Walcott, who kept wicket to him in his sensational triumph with Alf Valentine in 1950, admitted that he was often as perplexed as the batsmen.

I did not play for England until a year later, and my method in later series was to play him off the front foot as an off-spinner, a method adopted by Peter May and Colin Cowdrey in their record stand of 411 for the fourth wicket in the first Test at Edgbaston in 1957.

In the first innings Ramadhin had routed England on a perfect pitch with 7 for 49. England, 288 behind, were 113 for three. Ramadhin bowled and bowled and bowled – 588 balls in the second innings and 774 all told – and was never the same again, and I was left once again to reflect on that little gremlin on my shoulder. I was left out of the chosen party at Edgbaston, was lbw for a 'duck' by Roy Gilchrist at Lord's, and might have gone first ball to Frankie Worrell – the ball went close to backward-short-leg – in the next Test at Trent Bridge. That was at 11.40 a.m. on the Thursday and I was not out until 2.20 p.m. on Friday. In all I batted seven hours fifty-five minutes, for my highest score of 258. And neither Ramadhin nor Valentine took a wicket in the match.

Ramadhin was run out in the Leeds Test by David Sheppard, by then a man of the cloth, and when he returned to the pavilion, Valentine, his Calypso twin, received him with the words: 'Well, the Bible does say "Thou shall not steal"!' Peter May, Colin Cowdrey, Peter Richardson and I each scored two hundreds in the series, including two doubles and three in excess of 150 – nowadays that would be considered really exceptional.

The big difference between the West Indies sides of 1950 and 1957 was the decline of Ramadhin and Valentine. On their first visit they shared fifty-nine wickets in four Tests; and seven years later only fourteen – all to Ramadhin. But the West Indies are never down for long. The talent seems inexhaustible and, whenever their great gallery of fast bowlers is mentioned, I find myself wondering if it is fully appreciated just how good Sir Gary was in his role as new-ball opener. I would rate Sobers more dangerous with the new ball than either Wes Hall or Charlie Griffith, and when he went all out and slipped himself he could be just as fast, at least with the occasional delivery or over a short spell.

Gary Sobers and Australia's Alan Davidson were the two left-arm pace bowlers I most feared, and I can safely say my opinion would be shared by all their opponents around the world. Both had the priceless gift of being able to swing the ball into the right-hander with a late dip as well as making the odd one move away off the pitch. Normally the left-arm quick bowler goes across the body, which can be awkward enough, but another whole dimension is added to the batsman's problems if the ball comes back. Nothing is more worrying than to have to guard against talent which can be so diversified. Gary also disconcerted with the way he was able to make the ball swing and swerve, and mix in a bouncer or two.

Generally Gary wisely believed in a full attacking length. Geoff Boycott will not forget the incredible in-swinger he received at Trent Bridge in 1966, when Gary took the new ball specifically because he thought that if there was one chink in the Yorkshireman's armour it might be to the 'in-dipper' at the start of an innings. The ball started so wide that Boycott shaped to cut, but it bent back so much that he was leg before. Sobers had scored only three – and I was always particularly wary of his bowling if he had failed with the bat!

Alan Davidson reckons that the ball which dismissed me at Melbourne in the 1958-9 series was about the best he ever bowled, and I certainly would not challenge his opinion. It was an absolute beauty. Slanting in from eighteen inches outside the off stump, it would have hit the middle stump if I had not padded up in desperation. I read various descriptions of that dismissal – Peter Richardson, Willie Watson and I went in the course of six deliveries – and, strangely, most were critical of me rather than in praise of the bowler.

Another very awkward left-arm bowler was big Bill Johnston, who was the perfect support for Ray Lindwall and Keith Miller. Support implies a secondary role, but Bill was magnificent in his own right, swinging either way and very late with a lazy action – at least that's how it looked until you were just twenty-two yards away.

There was never a friendlier soul than Bill. During Bradman's 1948 tour of England, when the Australians were at

Oxford, he made friends with an undergraduate and his family. The next morning Bill found himself bowling to his new mate and, being a generous soul, aimed to give him one to get off the mark. To his dismay, however, the ball swung from leg to bowl the unfortunate victim, who had probably never had a delivery of similar quality before. As soon as it took off Bill threw up his arms in despair and, to the amusement of the Aussie fielders, shouted, 'Oh! . . . Sorry!'

I shall always have affectionate memories also of Keith Miller, the other member of the terrible triumvirate of Lindwall, Miller and Johnston, as well as Wes Hall. Miller was not just a crowd-entertainer and a magnetic personality, he was a very generous opponent. It scarcely needs saying that he was a magnificent three-in-one cricketer with his fast bowling, his batting – he always hankered to be a batsman rather than a bowler – and his slip catching, but behind that devil-may-care façade he was a deadly serious competitor. He never let a game die if he could help it, even if it meant rousing the spectators with a flurry of bumpers. 'Hey, what's going on?' I once demanded. 'Just for the mob,' he replied with a little cough, 'just for the mob.'

As handsome as a film star, Keith was a big man in everything he did, on and off the field, and his interests were as diversified as the turf and classical music. In fact he was too large a personality for the conventional authoritarians to understand, and he never captained Australia. More's the pity, perhaps, as neither did his old 'cobber', Denis Compton. Had those two been the opposing captains, any disputes would have probably been settled with a joke over a glass of beer. (Not that I conformed to the purist's conception of the thinking captain, either.) The tales of Keith's days as leader of New South Wales are legion, and have enlivened many a dressing-room.

Bobby Simpson told me of his first experience as a young player under the glamorous Keith. As they took the field Bobby was all agog to see what made the great man tick. He was, therefore, taken aback to hear the first command for field placings: 'OK, you guys, scatter!'

In another match an alert scorer noticed twelve players leaving the gate and making their way to the middle. On being told this by a breathless official, Keith, who did not have much time for such mundane matters as the final team selection, turned to his team and remarked, 'Well, in that case one of you had better buzz off.'

For all the stories, true and apocryphal, it would be quite absurd to dismiss the man who once turned up at Lord's for a Test still wearing his dinner jacket, as an irresponsible playboy. Believe me he could be deadly serious when the occasion demanded, but, like Compton, he was such a naturally gifted ball player that he could afford to go his own way, untrammelled by dull convention. Actually conformity acted as a challenge to Miller and Compton, and it was fascinating to observe, from the nonstriker's end, the sometimes almost leisurely, indifferent pose of Keith in the slips. His mind, it seemed, was far away, perhaps at Ascot or on the Melbourne Cup.

Give him half a chance, however, and he would take the type of catch to turn a match. His attitude befitted his open-hearted nature and, being so sublimely gifted with talent, temperament and physique, he scarcely needed to work at the game. In a sense he was at the opposite end of the spectrum to Geoff Boycott, who is the most dedicated player I have known.

I particularly warmed to Keith at Sydney in 1955 when I took Bill Edrich's place for the last Test. Hutton had clinched the Ashes, and there was a little feeling in my mind that here was my chance to prove myself after having missed the two previous Tests at Melbourne and Adelaide. Len went to the fourth ball he received, but the gods were with me and my drive worked swiftly. I am told Hutton commented: 'Why can't he always play like this?' If only cricketers knew the answer to that one! Eventually I took four boundaries in an over off Keith to reach my hundred – regrettably my only century off Australia – and there was Miller applauding every stroke and being the first to say 'Well done.'

Wes Hall was the same at Trent Bridge, 1966, following through non-stop and extending a huge fist after I had hooked him to the boundary. No one knows better than the cricketer the truth of the old saying, 'You can't win 'em all', and there is a genuine feeling of pleasure in sharing a well-earned success. Heaven knows there are failures a-plenty! I confess to being pleasurably surprised by a little story from Roy Lawrence, the noted Jamaican radio commentator then accompanying the 1963 West Indies side. As he was first to receive the news of England's team selection, he passed it on to the skipper Frankie Worrell. Always, Roy assured me, Worrell's opening query was, 'Is Graveney in?'

Quite apart from that, I always thought Worrell was the classiest batsman of the three W's. Everton Weekes and Clyde Walcott could be butchers with the bat, but Frankie would perform his execution of bowlers as if he had stepped out of the pages of a textbook. I was playing in the Barbados Independence match when his death was announced, and I have never seen so many grown men crying. He was a great man as well as a great cricketer, and the loss of his influence as a captain was felt in every corner of the game. Frankie, who had deep natural dignity, would never have allowed any lapse in the standards of decorum or discipline. He never had to bring out a stick, for the simple reason that he was too well respected.

The value of discipline was demonstrated by the South Africans, who, although given no chance, held Australia to a draw in 1952–3 and narrowly lost in England in 1955. In the second Test on a well-grassed pitch, I thought that Peter Heine and Neil Adcock were as hostile a pair as I have ever seen. Yet, oddly, Heine had been passed over for the first Test, and Adcock lost his place after breaking a bone in his foot. Nevertheless, Adcock was the first South African fast bowler to take a hundred Test wickets, and though he had a windmill action and did not use his body – I recall Bob Wyatt saying to me he couldn't be really fast without using his body – he was surprisingly quick. He ran in fast and stood up straight at the moment of delivery, and was at his best in 1961 when I was out of favour with the selectors.

As an opening batsman on that late June morning at Lord's, in 1955, I can testify that Heine's speed was like greased lightning. If that was not enough, it seemed to me, he wasn't all that interested in the stumps, as he was inclined to use them as direction finders rather than objects to aim at. Heine, over six foot four and proportionately built, had no objection to seeing his opponents wince – not that I blame him for that. The first ball of the match took off from a length and flew over Don Kenyon's head. Had I been a fast bowler, that alone would have put an extra yard on my pace. Both Peter May and Denis Compton were caught trying to get out of the way of savagely lifting deliveries, and the few runs I scored were as hard-gained as any I got.

May, who made 112, and I had revenge in the second innings with a stand of 132, and in the end Brian Statham took the first seven wickets in twenty-two overs for thirty-one runs, and England, who had been 171 runs behind, won by 71 runs. I still wonder what might have happened if Statham and Freddie Trueman had bowled on the first day. It was a fact of life that the pitches of that era were often dangerous. The fast attack is far from a modern invention!

It is trite to observe that no one really relishes authentic fast bowling, but batsmen have the right to demand fair conditions, and, above all, an even bounce. Nothing demoralises a side more than fast bowling aided by surfaces providing variable heights, and my heart went out to Mike Denness's side in Australia in 1974-5 when Dennis Lillee and Jeff Thomson, undeniably a redoubtable pair, had the advantage of sub-standard pitches. I am not suggesting for one moment that Lillee and Thomson would not have won the series on better wickets, but it must have made their success that much more certain. England sustained two injuries in the first Test, on the Brisbane pitch prepared by the amateur groundsman Clem Jones, and never really recovered. Even John Edrich, the most courageous of fighters, had had more than enough long before the end of the rubber. Nothing destroys a batsman's confidence more than an untrue bounce.

I remember only too well the special problems of a different nature provided by the old coir mat at Karachi Gymkhana in the days when Pakistan were seeking full Test status. Fazal Mahmood, formidable enough at any time, was nothing less than a magician on the mat. At about Tom Cartwright's speed he cut the ball viciously, either way, a matter of three or four inches, which meant that he was virtually a high-quality medium-paced spinner. There could not have been another bowler in the world like him on matting, so that a total of 200 took a lot of getting. My 123 at Lahore for MCC against Pakistan in an unofficial Test in 1951, therefore, gave me intense satisfaction, though Pakistan won by four wickets and their Test claim was upheld a year later.

I suppose that innings and an 118 off the West Indies at Port-of-Spain in 1968 against Wes Hall, Charlie Griffith, Gary Sobers and Lance Gibbs were as good centuries as I ever made. *Wisden* described my Trinidad effort as 'a glorious exhibition of cultured batting'. Oddly enough, while I realised that everything was going right with the execution of shots, timing, placements and so on, it wasn't until I reached the pavilion and the compliments started that it dawned on me that it had been one of those special days.

They were two innings which I would privately maintain made a mockery of the charge sometimes levelled against me that I was a 'fancy cap' batsman. There were no cheap runs to be had against the likes of Fazal Mahmood, who showed what he could do on a helpful turf pitch at The Oval in 1954, or Lance Gibbs. Just as Australia were fortunate to have Alan Davidson and Ron Archer to follow the Lindwall-Miller-Johnston dynasty, the West Indies were favoured with Lance Gibbs, after Sonny Ramadhin and Alf Valentine. I was brought up at Gloucestershire with off-spinners of the calibre of Tom Goddard, David Allen, John Mortimore and 'Bomber' Wells, and I think I could be regarded as something of a specialist in assessing the breed.

Lance Gibbs and South Africa's Hugh Tayfield were magnificent hard wicket off-break bowlers, but neither, in my opinion, matched the genius of Jim Laker. Tayfield relied heavily on the outstanding support he had in the field, particularly with his two forward-short-legs, and Gibbs only learned to bowl round the wicket during his years with Warwickshire. Lance spun quite a lot, managed bounce on hard wickets, and was a great competitor. He also liked to bowl his overs in a quick rhythm – so much so, that half-way through what looked like becoming a maiden the prudent batsman invented a minor stoppage, like readjusting a pad or examining the pitch. We had many a battle in Tests and in county games. Once, in a Test match, the ball was returned so quickly after I had been backing up that Lance had a chance to run me out.

It was towards the end of the day, and I was so tired that I said, 'You can do it if you like.' Lance merely grinned. I think that grin reflected the spirit which existed between Gibbs and all his rivals.

Laker was the complete master. He had everything: an ability to spin the ball as much as he wanted to – like a top, or just enough to deceive; an away drifter; and changes of flight and pace. In short, the lot. Without question he was by far the most difficult of English spinners to play against, and I don't think it was always appreciated how beautifully balanced he was in his delivery stride, an invaluable asset if he saw a batsman about to 'make the charge'. With a minor adjustment he could hold back his delivery until the last possible moment. I felt there was no future in trying to unsettle him. If proof was ever needed of his control, accuracy and bowling brain, it was provided during his one tour of Australia – yes, unbelievably, *one* tour, in 1958-9.

The Aussies had made no secret of their intention to extract full revenge for their annihilation by Jim in 1956 on what some of them described as 'ragbag' wickets; but on a disastrous tour he emerged top of the England bowling averages, both in Tests and for all his matches in Australia and New Zealand. Only once, by Neil Harvey at his superb best in the second Test at Melbourne, was Jim manhandled.

Before then South Australia – one guesses the adroit hand of Sir Don Bradman at work – had attempted to deflate Laker's reputation with an all-out assault on him. The ploy ended with Jim toying with the batsmen, taking 5 for 31 in the first innings and 5 for 70 in the second. Catches came to me at long-on, just as Jim promised they would. I scarcely needed to move an inch to take them, so precise was Jim's uncanny control, and I felt part of a conspiracy engineered by a master craftsman.

My advice to any aspiring off-spinner is to study every action photograph of Laker he can lay his hands on. Better still, old film clips, because nothing better can be seen. The value of a perfect action was brought home to me in a difficult light at Romford when Jim, then playing for Essex at the end of his illustrious career, bowled on a green pitch after the quick bowlers had gained nothing from the conditons. Yet, even at his pace, Jim was able to get the ball to lift at chest height. He was truly a great bowler. The main Surrey attack of Alec Bedser, with his deadly leg-cutter and later in-swing, Peter Loader, as hostile as anyone with the new ball, and the spinning twins of Tony Lock and Laker – well supported by Eric Bedser – must have been the most accomplished county attack of all time.

Alec Bedser's achievements for England were all the more creditable because, for most of his fifty-one Tests, he did it without a settled partner. Bowlers usually hunt in pairs, complementing each other's styles, but Bedser did it alone.

Another outstanding off-spinner was Freddie Titmus. He caused me a lot of problems with his use of the crease and a lovely, natural away-swinger. There was also a lesson for selectors to learn from the career of Richie Benaud. Probably only his robust batting kept him in the side, but he persevered with his leg-spin until his unquestioned talent began to emerge. He was not a big spinner of the ball, but his length and line seldom departed from strict accuracy. Indeed he was as accurate as an orthodox left-arm spinner. Benaud had a particularly good googly, and I always felt that his attitude, superbly demonstrated when he became one of Test cricket's most dynamic leaders, more than made up for any technical deficiencies. His aggression made you suspect that he thought it merely a matter of time before he got you out. Also, like Mike Brearley, he had the drive and personality to get the last ounce out of his players.

All things considered, I would rank Bruce Dooland, the Australian who went to Nottinghamshire, as a superior leg-spinner to Benaud. Bruce had a marvellous googly and flipper, as well as bounce and pace variations. Normally I loved the challenge of spin, and I boast that George Tribe, the left-arm googly merchant of Australia and Northamptonshire, did not cause me the sleepless nights he caused many county batsmen. By watching his hand I was able to sort out his various offerings so accurately that Keith Andrew, that polished wicket-keeper, now doing splendid work for the National Cricket Association, told me that George used to give me a run at the start of an over, so that he could bowl at the other batsmen.

The pair to give me the most trouble at county level were Derek Shackleton, of Hampshire, and Tom Cartwright, of Warwickshire. For over after over they nagged away, with a little bit of swing and a little bit of movement off the pitch, and always with an immaculate length. It was impossible to be ambitious against them, and they thrived on county pitches and English conditions. They were products of England's domestic cricket, which can be far removed from the cricket played on pitches prepared for Test matches and those encountered overseas. The medium-pacer, so useful at home, is normally out of his natural environment abroad, where the need is either to bowl at genuine speed or to spin the ball hard.

11
Bumpers, Helmets and Aggro

In my time I had my share of bumpers from some of the most fearsome bowlers in the world, like Ray Lindwall, Keith Miller, Peter Heine, Neil Adcock, Wes Hall, Charlie Griffith and Roy Gilchrist. I did not face Dennis Lillee and Jeff Thomson, nor obviously the present crop of West Indian giants, but I guarantee they were not faster than their predecessors. Maybe they bowl more bumpers in these times, encouraged as they must be by the sight of protective helmets and the batsmen's poor techniques against bouncers.

I knew exactly what it was like to see a potentially lethal missile hurtling towards my head at a speed fast enough to land a motorist in the dock, and I sensed the angry breath of the ball as it passed by. I heard, too, the excited whoops and whistles of crowds in the West Indies and Australia, and I sometimes asked myself if what they really wanted was blood. I have seen dressing-room pals and friendly rivals felled, and I shall never forget the panic dash to the Trinidad pavilion by Jim Laker, in 1954, after he had been hit in the eye by Frank King.

Nothing is more calculated to make the flesh creep or to raise blood pressures than bouncers. However, dangerous and emotive though the bouncer may be, the delivery in itself ought not to give any batsman worthy of the name undue concern, provided he is in the right position and keeps his nerve. And the only way to be in the right position is to keep the head perfectly still, with the eye on the ball all the way. The trouble is that batsmen do not obey the basic rule, and get into difficulties because they are on the move when the ball is bowled. Watch today's batsmen and you will notice that they fidget and shuffle.

I recently did a series of coaching films for Television South West with Somerset players, including Ian Botham, Viv Richards, Joel Garner and Brian Rose. Rose was aghast to see from the picture that he was doing a little bob up and down with his head during the ball's flight. He said he had never realised what he was doing and, like the exemplary professional that he is, he set about correcting the fault - with beneficial results.

I was interested to note Bill O'Reilly's confirmation of an opinion of mine in the *Sydney Morning Herald* after the 1982-3 series. He wrote that he was depressed to learn from Greg Chappell's century at Adelaide that Australia's best batsman was 'practically defenceless against the short-pitched ball'. With typical O'Reilly clarity, he added that he did not think there was one batsman on either the Australian or the England side who would earn five marks out of ten for hooking.

There is no shadow of a doubt that O'Reilly is right, and the modern batsman also falls into the trap of thinking he is obliged to hook a short-pitcher, even if it is pitched outside the off stump. This indeed is a dangerous fallacy. Hooking on or around the off stump is a hazardous and strictly un-professional enterprise, for if the stroke is fractionally mis-timed there is a real danger of the ball being deflected into the face.

Like so many of his contemporaries Don Wilson, late of England and Yorkshire and now the much-respected head coach at the Indoor School at Lord's, is appalled by the number of batsmen who are caught hooking at deep-fine-leg or deep-square-leg. This trap is quite obviously laid, and yet so many walk right into it. Not to put too fine a point on it, the batsman is a sucker to be a compulsive hooker and to be so easily 'thought out'.

Wilson feels this so strongly that he once declined to contribute to a coaching book on the theme of 'How to play the bouncer', because he believes the short answer is not to play it. Broadly speaking I am with him, and he is absolutely spot on to cite Reg Simpson as the prime example of his theory. Fred Rumsey, who bowled fast left arm for England and Somerset, and had a testing bouncer, adds his testimony by saying that he only ever gave Simpson one bouncer. Seeing Reg's almost contemptuous reaction, Fred gave it up as a waste of time. In short, Simpson's skill and attitude imposed his authority over a potentially dangerous opponent.

Simpson's method seemed disarmingly simple. He swayed out of line and allowed the ball to fly harmlessly by. When I batted with him for England, I recognised him as a past master of the art of dealing with the bouncer. He could hook all right, but only when he was satisfied everything was right, including the pace of the pitch, but otherwise he blandly but effectively discouraged any form of intimidation by swaying six inches one way or the other and not offering a stroke. The simplest methods are invariably the best, and analysing Reg's techniques against the short-pitcher one began to wonder what all the fuss was about. After a bouncer, which takes a lot out of a bowler, Simpson also had the habit of looking down the pitch as if to say: 'My, that must have been very hard work, and it hasn't disturbed me one iota.' It must have been a deflating experience for the bowler.

Wilson rightly argues that the persistent use of bouncers has done much to destroy off-side strokeplay – and consequently one of the beauties of the game – and denied spectators the thrill of spectacular slip catches. There cannot be any sensible argument in favour of methods which suffocate the finer arts and delights of cricket, and so complete has that suffocation been in recent series that, if Wally Hammond had been playing, it is likely that little of his classical off-side shots would have been in evidence. Most of his time at the wicket would have been spent fending off short-pitchers. The tactics would be to 'contain' him, and the bowlers would not pitch the ball up to him to drive.

As the successful hook against the bouncer is one of the most exciting shots – and has the element of claiming and exacting revenge – the main objection to the Wilson theory is that it would slow the tempo to a veritable crawl and bore spectators, who, in these times, demand instant action. Wilson says: 'Marvellous – then perhaps bowlers and captains would realise just how much their methods are harming the game.' A case of the end justifying the means. But perhaps if more batsmen perfected Simpson's method of playing the bouncer, bowlers would learn to use it more sparingly – as a surprise weapon rather than as a stock ball. This would be preferable to any attempt to legislate.

Experiments rationing bowlers to one bouncer an over have been reasonably successful, but I cannot see eager co-operation from countries like the West Indies and Australia, who have an abundance of pace, and in any case there are always arguments about the definition of a short-pitcher. Jeff Thomson, for instance, on the poor Australian pitches of 1974–5, made the ball climb in an alarmingly short distance, and here I would like to say that if the authorities cannot curb the number of bouncers then at least they must insist on better and fairer pitches. The batsman's curse is the pitch of uneven bounce – bad enough at all times but impossible with bouncers flying around.

Denis Compton, as always, had his own methods against bouncers and, as you might expect, he was marvellous. Though he always struck his pull shot with typical power – the absolute certainty of his strokeplay was as positive as his audacity – his hook was really only a 'help on', but such was his timing and positioning that he did not put himself in physical danger. The only occasion I recall him being hit was when he deflected a 'no ball' bumper from Ray Lindwall on to his forehead at Old Trafford in 1948 – the Test in which Len Hutton, incredible to relate, was dropped because it was felt his confidence had temporarily gone against the bouncers of Lindwall, Miller and Johnston. My Gloucestershire team-mate George Emmett took his place and himself fell to a short-pitcher from Lindwall, when he lost it and ended up pushing his bat out one-handed. Compton, incidentally, returned after a rest to score 145 not out, and England totalled 363. Without casting too many aspersions, I wonder how many a current England side would get against Lindwall, Miller, Johnston, Sam Loxton, Ernie Toshack and Ian Johnson, and with the new ball allowed after sixty-five overs!

Colin Cowdrey also moved inside the ball in the Compton fashion to 'help on' a bouncer but, unless you were a Compton, a Cowdrey, a Cyril Washbrook, who made a profitable speciality of the hook, or had the skill and courage of a Bill Edrich, you didn't automatically hook. The hook was reserved for only when it was considered fairly safe and the batsman was in the right position.

Since I retired from the first-class game, and especially since I have watched from the commentary box, I have been secretly amazed that, being predominantly a front-foot player, always edging into a forward position and thus moving into a bouncer, I was only hit once. The bowler was Pakistan's Khan Mohammad in a match at Lahore, and oddly I lost sight of the ball in the reflection from the pitch, which shone like polished glass. Fortunately I took only a glancing blow on the side of my head.

I had my ration of bouncers, not only in Tests, against Australia, the West Indies and South Africa, but on the home front too. John Snow and John Price in particular did not hold back against me, and Les Jackson, though not terribly quick, could be decidedly unpleasant. But it was Peter Loader who tended to give county batsmen sleepless nights. One such batsman was my Gloucestershire team-mate Martin Young, who, though he did take runs off Surrey, was worried sick before he was due to face Loader.

Loader, with a deceptive physique like a stick of rhubarb, was right in the top class, and I doubt if it is generally realised what demands he placed on his opponents. Arching his body like a bow to get maximum propulsion, he used the crease with all the guile of a slow bowler like Freddie Titmus, and he swung the ball either way like a boomerang at authentic speed. His bouncer leapt at the throat, but I have to say in all honesty that it was suspect. I cannot pretend I enjoyed meeting Peter at his best and it says a lot for the strength of England's bowling in the fifties that he was called upon for only thirteen Tests.

A little later, when pitches were on the rough side at Worcester, my second county possessed some formidable bumper men, led by Jack Flavell who, like Lindwall, seldom pitched the ball too short and yet could send it bouncing like a tennis ball high over the batsman's head. His slinging action ensured that he was spot-on – right at the throat!

Rubbish bouncers, dropped in the bowler's half of the pitch, may look spectacular, but as far as I was concerned they could bowl them all day. They didn't even arouse ill-feeling, but the bouncer at the throat is entirely a different matter.

The bouncers I feared most came from the fast left-arm bowlers Gary Sobers and Alan Davidson because, if they pitched it in the right place, as they invariably did, the ball went across my body in the direction of first slip. The slightest misjudgment might cause either a painful blow to the body or an edged catch. I never attempted to hook them unless they strayed down the leg side – and that was about as often as there are Christmas days in a year.

My special luck, I am sure, was to play against Mike Procter when he still only bowled over the wicket. Had I stayed in the game a little longer and faced him when he had perfected his attack from round the wicket, I have little doubt that his bumper would have been as difficult as any I handled, if not the most difficult of all. As it was, his highly individual style of bowling, 'off the wrong foot', made him hard to pick up, but he had to bowl wide of the crease. Consequently his bouncer, if pitched properly, went a little down the leg side and across the body, and it required only a fairly comfortable shot to help the ball on its way. Also, if directed at the batsman, it needed to be pitched so far outside the off stump that it did not require acrobatics to back away and let the ball go. When Mike changed the angle and directed the ball across the batsman from round the wicket, there were no such escapes.

For some reason I had an instinctive feeling, a kind of sixth sense, for a bouncer. I cannot begin to offer an explanation, but it served me as well as having a friendly guardian angel perched on my shoulder. Warning bells began to jingle in my head, and I can honestly say I was seldom caught unprepared, Take Wes Hall as an example. If I was offered a huge ransom to say why, I couldn't do so, but somewhere in his run-up something seemed to happen and I knew, just as if he had given a pre-arranged signal, that a bouncer was on the way.

I had no in-born telepathy against the unpredictable Keith Miller. I suspect he was not on the same wavelength as the rest of us ordinary mortals! Keith did run up faster for the bouncer, which Denis Compton, among others, thought was his give-away, but with his plunging run one could never be positively certain, perhaps because Keith himself might not have been sure of his own intentions. I had even seen a fast googly result from one of those plunging runs – one such victim was the current Anglican Bishop of Liverpool! It was that sort of caprice which, on top of his extravagant natural gifts, made Keith such a fascinating and difficult opponent. The orthodox bored Keith – he needed a challenge to stimulate him. Suddenly he would make an old ball swing far more than when it had its shine, and I have known him turn to me in mid-afternoon and say, 'I think the natives need waking up.' And he would indeed wake up players and crowd alike with an electric spell of bowling, laced with bumpers for the sheer hell of it.

Bumpers cannot be banned; nor should they be. Fairly used, they are a legitimate weapon to be used as a surprise, to test a batsman's skill and resolve, to unsettle and break concentration, and to try and induce a hurried and false stroke. In the recent past there have been far too many, and batsmen have not been given the protection of good wickets. Both the spirit and letter of the law, which could not be set out in plainer language, have been broken. Some bowlers have got away with murder, and when a character of John Edrich's undoubted spirit declares he has had enough, and when others not lacking in 'bottle' are said to be shell-shocked, it can be taken that the borderline of fair play and sanity has been over-stepped.

At the same time, I do not believe modern techniques are right. I also think that the helmet, now regarded as every bit as essential a piece of equipment as pads, thigh pads, gloves and protectors, actively encourages short-pitched bowling. Bowlers think they are absolved from responsibility for accidents, and that, as the helmet protects the head and face, they have a licence to let it rip. I can well imagine the helmet acting like a red rag to a bull to some bowlers. I can guess what Freddie Truman's reaction would have been. He certainly wouldn't have pitched the ball up, or I'm a Chinaman!

Before the war 'Patsy' Hendren produced a prototype of today's helmet, but he was such an incorrigible leg-puller that I was never sure whether he intended to be taken seriously. Mike Brearley and Dennis Amiss duly produced their own versions, and if helmets give confidence, that is fair enough. Having tried one on, however, there is no way I could have played in a helmet. To me a helmet is strange, cumbersome, hot and heavy. Maybe it is a matter of usage and habit, but I would prefer to take my chance.

If a batsman is good enough he does not need a helmet, and it is significant that neither India's superb Sunil Gavaskar, a target for the bouncer if there ever was one, nor the incomparable Viv Richards, bothers with a helmet – for the obvious reason that they have confidence in themselves. They can get into the right positions to deal with any bouncer.

Obviously even if I were a cricket dictator, I would not ban the helmet for batting, but I certainly would not allow it in the field, as it patently gives an unfair advantage.

Since adopting the helmet, close-in fielders on both sides of the wicket have gone two yards closer to the bat, with a better chance of taking the bat-pad catches and the tiny snicks, and without fear of serious injury. Nor are they likely to be forced to retreat by the time-honoured method of a few well-struck blows by a determined batsman. The protected fielder can now cock a snook at batsmen, and there will come a time when the batsman is surrounded by figures looking as if they have stepped straight from a space-ship. Already some fieldsmen are protected (sensibly enough) by soccer shin-guards tucked inside the socks. The next development could be pads for silly-mid-offs, and, in the course of time, fielders will begin to look like American grid-iron footballers.

We have reached the absurd position in which Law 23, dealing with catches, has had to embrace notes to cover the ball lodging in a helmet, and touching a helmet. Times have indeed changed!

While I would unhesitatingly ban helmets in the field, it is clearly impossible to legislate in the contentious area of bouncers against tail-end batsmen. For generations it was an un-written rule that those least able to defend themselves from the bumper should be spared, but like many other conventions it has gone by the board. There have been several instances of Number 11's taking bouncers. There is usually the excuse that it was an accident, or that the batsman had been at the wicket long enough; sometimes even an argument over the actual length of the delivery.

In general terms I still think it common sense not to bounce at tail-enders, but there can be the case of the late batsman, who, knowing the ball is going to be pitched up to him, pushes forward with assurance and successfully defends his wicket. Not many teams these days would let a Number 11 get away with that in the last ten minutes of a Test, when no holds are barred.

Players, not committees, should sort out these situations,

but alas, the old, sensible, healthy competition has been replaced by downright aggression and an obsession to win not
entirely explained by the rich pickings of Test cricket.
Cricket, it has been widely noted, invariably mirrors the
moods and manners of the times, and possibly the emphasis
on bouncers, functional helmets, which seem to strip players
of their personalities, making them hard to identify and de-
humanising the game, and the general lack of on-field discipline, is not out of place in the aggressive eighties.

One bouncer I shall never forget, because of the contrasting
personalities involved, was bowled by George Lambert, a
Gloucestershire stalwart, against 'Gubby' Allen, by then
making only occasional appearances for Middlesex, in the
security of the Cheltenham festival! George, a cockney, had
been on the Lord's staff and he gave 'Gubby' an awkward
bouncer to which he got the bat handle in the way in the nick
of time – only to be caught behind. Of course there was no
earthly reason why a bumper should not have been bowled at
'Gubby', who was still more than a useful performer. But I
don't think I would have been too pleased if I had been in his
shoes!

12
Vintage Players

My greatest regret is that I never saw Bradman play, and Hammond only once. In his four visits to England, Bradman only once went to Bristol – in 1930, when he was twice dismissed by the slow left-arm spinner Charlie Parker, and a sensational match ended in a tie. Bristol was never to see him again, but I was brought up in dressing-rooms where the names of Bradman and Hammond were held in awe, and I would have given much to have been at first slip to a batsman who, I have been repeatedly assured by the best judges, had a shot for every ball. The rate at which Bradman accumulated his runs proved his mastery. The older bowlers say that they often did not realise they were being taken apart all that much, but they would glance at the scoreboard and be surprised at the runs he had collected.

It is still being argued whether or not Alec Bedser found a chink in that extraordinary armour when he dismissed him five times in a row, three of them caught in the backward-short-leg position by Len Hutton. Bradman was, of course, at the end of his unique career, but Bedser did bowl to a plan based both on his devastating in-swinger, which moved so late as to be almost posthumous, and his accuracy on the off stump. If the delivery on a full length was pitched exactly right, Bradman had to offer a forward stroke, with the prospect of a nick going to backward-short. And that happened three times – surely too often to rule out flukes.

The very presence of a master batsman can influence the pattern of a match, as I found out to my cost on the one occasion I played with Hammond, even though it was in the friendly serenity of a benefit game at Torquay. I had made 30 or so in reasonable style when he came in, and for no accountable reason I started to play like an idiot. The bowlers, too, were similarly affected and they included Khan Mohammad, who was experienced enough. What Hammond must have thought of his young partner, who was beginning to be talked about as a prospect, I can't imagine, but I felt like crawling away.

Unquestionably Hammond went on one tour too many when England were persuaded to go to Australia in 1946-7 after only one season of domestic cricket following the wartime shut-down. From all accounts, Hammond was a bit hard to get to, especially if you were a young player, but I would have given anything to have batted with him and to study him at close hand. I revelled in the stories of Hammond handed down in the dressing-room. Once Gloucestershire's main bowlers could not part the last pair. 'Give it to me,' he declared impatiently – and immediately produced a googly to end the match.

After a match at Cheltenham just after the war, Hammond was scathing in his criticism of the opposition, who had collapsed against Tom Goddard on a turning wicket. The great 'Wally' was in a leg-pulling mood and declared he could play Goddard on the same pitch with the edge of his bat. The challenge was taken up, and Goddard bowled to Hammond with his normal field assembled. Hammond showed the edge of his bat to the bowler and for half an hour or so he not only survived comfortably but did not make an error.

By modern standards Hammond's 2lb 4oz bat was light. Today some players use 3lb bats to (as they say) counter short pitches, and they argue that more power comes from a heavy bat. Personally I see no sense in that, as everything depends on positioning and timing.

★   ★   ★

Perhaps because of those post-match discussions we used to have over our beer, I am unable to resist picking teams, and here I am again thinking of the best I have played with and against, who would form my supreme England and World XI's. The time-scale excludes Bradman and Hammond, who would normally be the first two choices, and I judge my players at their peak form. Here is my England selection:

> Sir Len Hutton (capt.)
> John Edrich
> Peter May
> Denis Compton
> Colin Cowdrey
> Ian Botham
> Godfrey Evans
> Jim Laker
> Freddie Trueman
> Tony Lock
> Alec Bedser
> 12th man: Ted Dexter

Yes, I realise only too well that Geoff Boycott and Brian Statham and Frank Tyson and Bob Appleyard and Trevor Bailey and Ken Barrington, etc, etc, etc, are not there, which in no way diminishes my profound respect for their enormous contribution to Test cricket. In my opinion, Hutton, May and Compton are 'musts', and I have a fractional preference for Cowdrey over Dexter because I am agreeably haunted by that innings of astonishing brilliance that Colin played at Melbourne on Hutton's victorious tour of 1954-5. Not even Dexter at his most imperious – and few have struck the ball more sweetly – could quite reach Colin's supreme level. Colin could be cussed, but in technique and natural ability he can never be seriously placed in anything but the highest level.

Boycott has often been his own worst enemy and, no doubt, he would dismiss me as too casual. If Geoff had not been so ultra-careful, he would have walked into any England side, but on balance I go for the ideal opening partnership of

right- and left-handers which is inclined to upset the line of
bowlers. John Edrich, like his cousin Bill, was a byword in
determination, and a gutsy left-hander can be invaluable if
things should go wrong or to soften up the attack for the more
elegant stroke-makers.

Ian Botham would have my vote before Trevor Bailey as
the all-rounder, being the more challenging, positive batsman and more likely to win a match – indeed to turn it round
in a short space of time. Trevor put immense thought and
intelligence into everything he did, a quality which, reinforced by his quiet determination, ensured the maximum
use of his ability. I could never, by the very nature of my
temperament, steel myself to play the type of 'barnacle' innings for which he was famous, and I never thought he was
given the credit that was his due in the legendary partnership
with Willie Watson to save the Lord's Test in 1953. Willie
maybe rightly grabbed all the attention, but the result would
not have been possible without Trevor.

Bailey adopted a style to meet England's needs, and he was
a most valuable member of the team during Hutton's
triumphs, taking 100 wickets and scoring 2,000 runs in a
ten-year span. If he goes down in history as a slow-scoring
batsman, it will be a rank injustice, paying scant heed to his
outstanding bowling. England cannot have had, at any time,
a more dedicated team man.

What Botham means to England was vividly illustrated by
successive series against Australia. He was a spectacular success in 1981, when England won, and, judged by his own
standards, a relative failure in 1982-3, when England lost.
He has to be in my team.

My bowling would be spearheaded by Bedser, Trueman
and Botham, with the combination of Lock and Laker, who
should never be split, as the spinners – and with Compton,
able to contribute both orthodox and unorthodox slow left
arm, in support if necessary. With Bedser in the team, the
wicket-keeper must be Godfrey Evans, who in any case was
unsurpassed. Bedser liked his wicket-keepers to stand up

and, from my privileged position at slip, I never ceased to wonder at the best of Evans taking the best of Bedser. It was classical stuff.

Trueman was probably more pugnacious than Statham, though, as I have already said, Statham gave me more trouble. Laker has no serious rival as the off-spinner, and Lock's fielding steals him the advantage over his near rivals, led by Johnny Wardle. When the balance of England's attack was questioned on account of the inclusion of three off spinners, in Australia in 1982–3, I remember thinking it would not have been so bad if the three had been three Lakers! But that's an impossible thought.

For my World XI, I nominate:

> Sir Len Hutton (capt.)
> Barry Richards
> Viv Richards
> Denis Compton
> Neil Harvey
> Sir Gary Sobers
> Bruce Dooland
> Godfrey Evans
> Ray Lindwall
> Jim Laker
> Alec Bedser
> 12th man: Keith Miller

Again so much extravagant talent is left out. Had I been able to squeeze in Sir Frankie Worrell, he could have been captain – or for that matter, Richie Benaud. But I am obliged to use my own judgement, and Dooland, of Australia and Nottinghamshire, was the best leg-break and googly bowler I ever played against. In another age, when the emphasis might have been on spin rather than pace, Dooland's huge ability would have been better recognised.

Hutton was a sounder and more far-sighted tactician than Sobers; I don't think a team would go far wrong under him. The old grey fox knew what he was about, and, as was proved at Barbados, he was big enough to change his attitude if it was shown to be wrong. He shouldered massive burdens and emerged the victor in the long run, and I doubt if there would be many to dispute his position at Number 1. His partner could have been Sunil Gavaskar, Bert Sutcliffe or Hanif Mohammad, but I go for Barry Richards. To my mind Barry had just a little bit extra. Viv Richards unhesitatingly goes in first wicket down, and out of the purple ranks of the middle order Compton emerges edging in front of May, Pollock and any of the W's. All those were agonising omissions, as was Zaheer Abbas and Martin Donnelly. In fact, I suppose two more teams of equal strength and attraction could comfortably be chosen. Compton, again, could reinforce the spin of Laker and Dooland. It should not be forgotten that he was also a remarkably fine fielder.

Neil Harvey, Australia's champion after Bradman, is another automatic selection for me, followed by Sobers. Great as Miller, Wes Hall, Adcock and the rest were as opening bowlers, the two to emerge to use the new ball in my opinion are Lindwall and Bedser. If the conditions suited Bedser he was, as Bradman insisted, as formidable as it is possible to imagine, with his leg-cutter virtually a fast leg-break. Lindwall, the complete fast bowler, has to be in, and with Sobers as first change, there is a fast attack which I wouldn't care to meet too often. Dennis Lillee is another possible, and there are also Alan Davidson, Ian Botham, Imran Khan and Kapil Dev left on the sidelines.

Yet I believe my side could meet all challengers in normal conditions, and even if some may think it's as well that I'm not a Test selector, to judge from my choice, at least it's fun to play around with ideas!

13
Cricket's South African Tragedy

One of the saddest and most incomprehensible moments of my cricket life came one evening in August 1968 in the peaceful surroundings of the Worcester pavilion, when a voice on the radio read the names of sixteen players chosen by England to tour South Africa. We had assembled ready to celebrate the inclusion of my team-mate and friend Basil D'Oliveira, recently one of England's heroes with a score of 158 in the victory over Australia at The Oval. As I had played a small part in his recall for that historic match, and I knew what it meant to him to return to his homeland as a symbol of hope for his fellow non-whites, I felt I had a personal stake in his selection. My mind went back to the time when I had persuaded him to try his luck in county cricket – with Worcestershire! Moreover I would have staked a second mortgage on his selection, particularly as he had been as good as told after his innings at The Oval that he was a certainty for the tour.

I could scarcely believe my ears when Bas was not mentioned. I was so flabbergasted that I was convinced a mistake had been made. I saw the pain of disappointment in Dolly's eyes, and all he said was: 'The stomach has been kicked out of me.' For a moment he was lost, and he would have been less than human if he had not suspected that he was once again the victim of politics. As the selectors were honourable men, Dolly accepted fully – as I did – the later statement that the omission was entirely on cricketing grounds, but equally I found it incomprehensible that Dolly was not considered to be among the first sixteen cricketers in the country.

Doug Insole, Chairman of Selectors, explained that Basil was regarded a batsman rather than an all-rounder for an overseas tour. Therefore, he had to be judged alongside the seven specialist batsmen. Also omitted was Colin Milburn. Perhaps it could be argued that Basil had never played better for England than he did at The Oval, and that he had not been a success in the West Indies. But at that point he had scored two centuries and seven fifties and averaged 50 in twenty-four Tests. Methinks England would like a Number 6 batsman of similar consistency in the eighties!

It is now a part of black history that when D'Oliveira subsequently replaced the unfit Tom Cartwright, the then South African Prime Minister Mr Jon Vorster broke the eighty-year-old cricketing links by banning the South African, in a political speech described in a *Daily Mail* leader as 'crude and boorish'. MCC were obliged in late September to cancel a tour which they could not undertake under such a condition. D'Oliveira was the innocent victim of politics. South Africa were banished, and the wretched business has dragged on ever since.

The issues have inevitably become so fudged with prejudice, malice and distortion on all sides that unless a solution is found soon the very fabric of cricket will be destroyed. Only a mischievous idiot would want to see the game divided into two implacably hostile and irreconcilable camps of black and white, with England, Australia, South Africa and New Zealand on one side of the barricade and the West Indies, India, Pakistan and Sri Lanka on the other. Such a situation would be stark tragedy, but unless some politicians show a little concern the worst could happen.

Viv Richards would have many nodding agreement with him, when he said in a newspaper interview, 'Politics is a dirty business, no matter what side you're on. It is up to every cricketer to decide the best way to fight apartheid, but

I think it was a mistake for Graham Gooch and the others to go' – a reference to the unofficial English expedition to South Africa immediately after the official tour of India in the Spring of 1982, which ended with all the players being suspended from Test cricket for three years – a loss of talent England could ill afford. Richards added, 'They were used – used to make the South African system look better.'

Since then, players from Sri Lanka and the West Indies have toured South Africa for contracts which make my earnings, and those of my contemporaries, look like small change. There have been extraordinary stories of cloak-and-dagger visits by South African cricket emissaries; of false passports and numbered Swiss bank accounts; of huge funds at the disposal of sporting authorities; players banned, and threats and counter-threats. Even a women's cricket team was refused entry by the West Indies in 1983 simply because some of their number had been to South Africa. There is a fatuous so-called United Nations black list, and heaven knows what else. A South African delegation, who wanted to put their case that the International Cricket Conference's stipulation of multi-racial cricket had been fulfilled, was denied even a hearing. It is not hard to guess who was responsible for what must be a profound error of judgement, goading South Africa to make even greater efforts to end their isolation by whatever means in their power. Even the more liberal elements of society, desperate to see the end of apartheid in any form, are afraid that some Governments are overplaying their hands.

As a simple cricketer, I abhor the intrusion of power politics into the game, and I am certainly not in favour of racial discrimination. I have too many genuine friends in the game, both black and white, to harbour doubts on that score. I want to see all cricketers everywhere allowed to play the game of their choice without being accused of supporting repressive regimes, or of taking blatantly extreme stances either way. I want to see an end to the sickening hypocrisy and double standards of Governments, who use sport and cricket for their own ends. An impossible middle-of-the-road position?

Perhaps, but the alternative is to see the greatest of all team games mangled and torn to pieces.

To me the worst aspect is the intevention of the politicians, beginning, if you like, with Mr Vorster. Sport is the easiest of targets, a soft option. We cry to heaven about the iniquities of apartheid, call on all sportsmen to sever all links, yet continue to trade, importing and exporting, and to invest in South Africa. About fifty-five per cent of foreign investment in South Africa comes from Britain, and exports to that country topped a billion pounds in 1980, an increase of forty per cent in ten years. So while the exporters and investors wax fat and grow rich, it is a 'crime' even for a county cricketer to spend six months in South Africa coaching whites, blacks and browns. At least Guyana thought it so when they banned Robin Jackman and stopped a Test match in a wrathful gesture of indignation.

In 1972 a delegation from the ICC went on a fact-finding tour of South Africa to see for themselves if the cause of multi-racial cricket had progressed, but it was a measure of the size of the problem that the only countries represented were England, Australia, New Zealand and the associated ICC members of the United States and Bermuda. The Commission recommended sending an international team as a first step, with all the profits going towards helping the cause of multi-racial cricket. That was the end of that! In passing, I have never quite appreciated why an action by cricketers in South Africa should threaten either the Olympics or the Commonwealth Games, since cricket is not concerned with either occasion.

If anyone has a right to express an opinion it is D'Oliveira, who learned his cricket under the crudest privations imposed by apartheid. His early games were played on matting laid on caked mud, and held down by boulders. The 'outfield' was rough, unkempt wasteland. Bare patches were interspersed with tufts of long grass, rocks and even electric power lines. Not far away was the beautiful Newlands ground, with its background of Table Mountain, a tree-lined avenue by one boundary, its lush grass and perfect pitch, and its facilities for whites only. Basil's way of learning to cope with the bouncer was to have helpful friends hurling a tennis ball down a flight of steps to him in the street below. Such was the background of a man of simple dignity who was destined to play forty-four times for England.

D'Oliveira went to South Africa, in January 1980, with a Sports Council delegation headed by former England Rugby International Dickie Jeeps. 'I thought it was my duty, as sport has done so much for me, to do something in return to help sportsmen of all beliefs and colours,' he told me. 'I saw much that was encouraging, but felt the isolation policy should continue for a few years yet, because I think it has helped the cause of non-racialism.'

There can be no argument that enormous progress in breaking down the sporting barriers has been made, and continues to be made, but the laws of the land remain unchanged except in minor respects. A black or brown cricketer is equal to a white on the field now, but as soon as the game is over he is subject to the apartheid laws. He is obliged to travel from the ground in a 'blacks only' compartment of his train.

'I walked round the cities as often as I could on that trip,' Dolly went on, 'and you couldn't miss the manifestations of apartheid. In Johannesburg, for instance, there were separate toilets and restaurants at both the airport and railway station.

'Various laws which prevent people of different colours mixing after sports events are gradually being ignored, though it only needs a complaint by one white man about coloured presence to force the police to take action.

'And there is still the permit system, where a black has to seek permission to join a white colleague in a bar or restaurant. That rankles, because things like free association would be taken for granted in Britain.

'I don't feel sorry that so many white South African cricketers have missed out on a Test career that must have been their ambition. How can I, when so many of my own race have been deprived of the chance even to play the game in proper conditions, let alone reach international level?

'The biggest divide has been in education, which is the first priority. Kids don't care about colour bars, and if the schools are properly integrated, then will come the time to welcome South Africa back to the sports community.'

I always have a feeling that observers like myself can only put a tentative toe into the deep-swirling waters of international politics. Cricket is caught up by the tides of big business, race, prejudice and intolerance, and the question is: can the game survive such intolerable pressures? If I had an answer I would be an oracle, but I do believe no impediment should be put in the way of encouraging South Africa to take steps to end their isolation. The danger of outlawing them indefinitely is to invite them to be even more reactionary and undo all the recent achievements. On that score I do not totally condemn the unofficial tour by Graham Gooch and Co., though I do not like the way they went about it.

But Dolly, whose opinion needs to be respected, disagrees. He says: 'The Government regards any such tour as upholding the present system. I hope the players didn't go there with any grandiose ideas about building bridges. They were there purely for the money, and in that respect alone I don't blame them. But I wonder what the West Indies people thought of Alvin Kallicharran and his winter coaching engagement in Johannesburg. True, he was with a multi-racial set-up, but they had to dip him and his family in whitewash for him to be accepted.'

Since then, of course, South Africa have succeeded in attracting unofficial teams from Sri Lanka and the West Indies, causing jubilation or dismay, according to one's political stance. The ramifications of such adventures spread wide and deep. The players involved can count their considerable booty at leisure, for their careers, at least in their homelands, are effectively over. Also, when the English team went, the immediate home series with India and Pakistan was threatened. Had those official tours not taken place, the counties would have been deprived of their share in the overall profits, and the television and radio contracts would have been dishonoured.

I am obliged to think the lesson which has to be learned by all Test-playing countries and their Governments is that the solution to the problem lies in corporate decisions, and that sooner or later they will have to face that problem squarely if the international game is not to be severed beyond repair. Those loudest in their condemnation of visits by English, West Indian and Sri Lankan teams, with their cries of 'blood money', should reflect that they might not have taken place at all if an official ICC multi-racial side had toured when the imaginative recommendation was made, or if the South African delegation had been given a hearing at the Conference meeting.

It should also be clearly understood that England and Australia in particular have made big sacrifices, in both financial and friendship terms, in standing by the principles of multi-racial cricket in South Africa. Others have merely paid lip service to the cause. Personally, knowing the passion for cricket in India and the West Indies, I would not care to be a politician in one of those countries whose action led to the future loss of Test matches and tours. To me it is unthinkable that political bigotry and brinkmanship could bring about a situation in which the West Indies would cease to tour Australia and England – the very two countries they look to for the financial solvency of their game.

I suppose it is asking too much for the throttling hand of politics to relax its grip on cricket's windpipe, but for the sake of the game, my old mate Dolly, Everton Weekes, Roy McLean and all the others of all shades and cultures, I sincerely hope that a speedy and lasting solution is found which will allow the game we all love to breathe freely again.

One of the supreme tragedies of cricket in recent decades has been the banishment from the international scene of South Africa's most talented players. All genuine lovers of the game,

irrespective of the arguments over apartheid and the continuing ban by the International Cricket Conference, unite in
lamenting the absence of Graeme Pollock, Barry Richards
and Mike Procter – to name but three of the many outstanding cricketers produced by South Africa.

Graeme, the left-handed batting genius, and his fast
bowling brother Peter, were able to give telling but all too
brief demonstrations of their gifts; but, sadly, the Test
careers of Richards and Procter were over almost as soon
as they had begun – eleven appearances between them.
What an outrageous waste! There can be no knowing just
how good they might have been. But I think I can hazard a
good guess.

In an era of often depressing mediocrity, Graeme Pollock's
genius was allowed to wither in South Africa's domestic
competitions, denying hours of pleasure to millions around
the world, all because of sport's exposure to the crossfire of
the politicians. What a loss it would have been if, for example,
Frank Woolley's career had been confined to twenty-three
Tests over a six-year span, and for the remainder of his time
he had been confined to the county championship and odd
encounters with sub-strength touring teams, which has been
Graeme's lot.

I have already referred to Mike Procter's bouncer, but
that, of course, was only part of the armoury of one of the
finest all-rounders of his generation. I first met Procter and
Richards at Cheltenham when they were trying to break into
county cricket. Unfortunately for Gloucestershire, they
couldn't hold on to both and Richards went to Hampshire –
otherwise large slices of county cricket history might well
have been re-written. As well as being a front-rank fast bowler, Procter, though not a reliable starter, was a brilliant
striker of the ball and almost as powerful as Ian Botham. At
the end of one season, when Gloucestershire had nothing to
play for except to entertain the public, Procter set out to score
the fastest century of the season. Normally not even the very
best batsmen start an innings with that deliberate intention.

It is one of those things that tend to happen. The gods smile down and suddenly everything clicks.

Yet Procter almost achieved his goal, with a flurry of controlled hitting, against opponents who certainly were not co-operating. Procter had the magic, shared by Botham, Miller and Sobers, to lift any occasion to sublime heights.

South Africa's cricketers of my generation have often been strong physically. Graeme Pollock's upright stance enabled him to hit the ball with force on the up off the front foot, and Barry Richards was also upstanding. Theirs were styles which obviously appealed to me. Richards also stood absolutely still and, if ever he hit across the ball, a fault which causes the downfall of so many contemporary English and Australian batsmen, it escaped my notice.

Barry Richards and Graeme Pollock must rank as the finest ever to come from South Africa. At the end of his stay with Hampshire, however, Richards became patently bored and disillusioned. I prefer the memory of a rampant Richards making the best bowling look ordinary – a fifty could almost be guaranteed on a Sunday, if television cameras were present – to the seemingly apathetic figure walking around the field with hands in pockets. In 1978 he left Hampshire with five matches to go, and it was obvious that the sheer weight of cricket sorely tried him at times. Even after his first season Barry confessed to strain and said he did not know how players kept going year after year. He told *Wisden*: 'I used to wake up in the morning and say to myself, "Not another day's cricket!" The strain is immense.'

14
Days when Botham did not Smile

English cricket will never be able to meet the debt it owes to Ian Botham. Those who say he is only a giant in an age of pigmies find no support from me, though it must be beyond argument that the 1981 Australians were a bad side, badly led. Botham has the talent of genius and there is not an England side since 1946 which would not have welcomed him with open arms. His impact would have been as great in any era, and it is a measure of his standing that he is deemed to have 'failed' even when he produces figures that other all-rounders would be pleased to have.

There have been few able to take a game by its ears and shake it into exciting life, as Ian is capable of doing in a sensationally short space of time. Just listen to the buzz of anticipation when he goes in to bat, or takes the ball. He is unconventional, uninhibited, throbbing with vitality and life, and to the desperately frustrated Australians of that unforgettable summer he must have appeared as a Churchillian bulldog – that is, once he was let off the leash. Botham, once freed from the captaincy, played for Mike Brearley with all the might he will give to a captain he respects.

Without wishing to appear wise after the event, I never understood why Botham was made captain. It is true that he was not being asked to do more than other all-rounders like Richie Benaud, Sir Gary Sobers, Sir Frankie Worrell and Ray Illingworth had successfully done before him. And it is equally true that the choice of Alec Bedser and his selectors was dreadfully restricted, and that there was a minimum of criticism when the appointment was made.

But I never saw the free spirit of Botham being tied to the cares of office. He has always been one of the boys, and, without a hint of disrespect, I doubt if he has had much to do with looking after himself, let alone ten others. I cannot picture him as a forward planner, a tactician in the mould of Hutton or Illingworth, a manager and inspirer of men like Brearley, or being patiently answerable for tactics which might have gone wrong. Men of action can also find the obligatory press conference and television interview a chore. For Ian the fun is relaxing in the dressing-room with a glass of ale and the chat of fellow players.

I did not believe it was prudent judgement for the selectors to chance promoting the best player in the side merely because he was the best player. The prospect of his form disappearing under the weight of responsibility was too severe a risk to take, especially as he led a moderate side against the West Indies, the strongest in the world, in successive series, home and away. Had he started off with a less daunting opposition, it might have been a different story. Again he was badly let down by missed chances in the opening Test at Trent Bridge in 1981. For England to lose in conditions so favourable to the home side was hard to take.

His own form, so essential to England's strength, went to pot, and inevitably the knives were out, and a scowling, unfamiliar cloud of failure darkened his career.

Significantly I did not see him smile once while he was captain. That was not Ian Botham. Enjoyment of his cricket is his hall-mark, and I am sure he would leave the game if it became a routine job to pay the rent. Quite simply Ian just wants to enjoy himself.

If a scriptwriter had invented the range of emotions experienced by Ian in one short summer, he would have been charged with lack of realism. There was the nadir of his career at Lord's, the drama of a fallen hero disappearing to boos on bagging a 'pair'. The loss of the captaincy against a background of sharpening knives, and on to dazzling triumph. What he did for the image of cricket is incalculable, and if anyone should make out his earnings are too high I would give an unprintable answer.

Once Botham was released from the burden of responsibility, and Brearley took it on, the series became folklore, an imperishable legend. The chemistry between the two was remarkable. Brearley has the magic touch, a deep understanding of human nature, and Botham and the entire England side responded to him like an orchestra to a maestro.

There was no better evidence than in the Edgbaston Test. England were not quite in the straits they had been in the furious match at Headingley, but it was desperate enough, with Australia needing only 142 to win and two days to get the runs. They were 105 for four, with a paltry 37 to score, when Brearley, about to use Peter Willey's off-spin, changed his mind and called up Botham.

For once Ian was not keen. He had just seen John Emburey make the ball lift and turn to dismiss Alan Border, and he undoubtedly felt, as Brearley himself had initially, that England's last slim chance lay in spin. 'No, I don't think I ought to bowl,' he said.

Many a captain would have shrugged his shoulders and left it at that, but I suspect Brearley, knowing Botham as well as Botham knows himself, sensed he had only one bowler in the situation. It was the perfect stage for Botham.

'Yes, have a go,' urged Brearley.

I noticed at once that Ian went in faster and was quicker than I had seen him for some time. The light of battle was in his eyes. His cricketing instincts told him that it was no time for experiments or wasteful bumpers, and he was deadly straight with a full length. In twenty-eight deliveries he had five wickets – three bowled, one lbw and the other caught at the wicket – for a single, and England had won by 29 runs.

Coming on top of his unbeaten 149 at Headingley, when England followed on 227 behind and were in actual danger of a second successive innings defeat, this was an outrageous drama. At one stage in the Headingley Test England were 135 for 7, 92 in arrears and, with Graham Dilley as his partner, Botham took the eighth wicket to an invaluable 117 in eighty minutes. The match was finally won by Bob Willis with his 8 for 43, but the odds of 500 to 1 against England offered at one point by Ladbrokes were not absurd. Most of the England side and television commentary team who had checked out of hotels would have agreed that the odds were about right. There was some hasty re-booking during the course of the afternoon!

I have to say that Kim Hughes' captaincy was poor and, like Graham Yallop in a previous series, he was no match for Brearley, who must rank as one of the finest captains of all time. The very fact that he was so far ahead at Headingley might have betrayed Hughes. Obviously he did not believe there was an escape route for England, and I doubt if he thought Dilley, as a late-order batsman, likely to be capable of giving Botham prolonged support. Logically he had one end open, but unimaginatively he persisted with his quick bowlers when he could have seen what Ray Bright, his left-arm spinner, had to offer. Australia had so much in hand that Bright would have been a very small gamble. He could have bowled into the rough to the left-handed Dilley, a ploy which could have taxed a batting specialist, let alone an inexperienced Number 9. Botham, too, would have responded by attacking Bright, which means he would have been liable to mistakes.

One of the remarkable facts of the partnership was that it was free of error. Not a single catch was offered. Botham was marvellous; Dilley, in his own way, became a titan; and amid the mounting Australian disarray Hughes was found seriously wanting.

I blush to think how close England came to being beaten by the worst Australian side I have ever seen. Had there not been the type of escape you expect no more than once in a decade if you are lucky – but here were two in one short summer – English cricket would have been destitute, out on the floor and with no foreseeable hope of recovery. As it was, public interest, which was fast dying away until the later stages of the Headingley Test, suddenly erupted and cricket was alive and well again.

The letters flooding into the commentary boxes were certain proof of a revival. Casual television viewers, who admitted to having no previous interest in the game, were converted to cricket's drama. That is one important reason why I insist there is an immeasurable debt owing to Botham!

Botham emerged from ordeal and triumph a more disciplined cricketer, certainly as a batsman. There was a time when he would go to the wicket very much as a slogger. If the ball was within reach he would have a go, but he is now far more responsible. It would not surprise me to see him give up bowling once he reached some personal target he has set himself – perhaps 350 Test wickets, or to pass the existing record. As he has got older his bowling has at times lost its edge, and being a little overweight he cannot get far enough round to bowl his outswinger. The shoulder needs to be pointing up the wicket, with the ball running away naturally. He has to work to get himself round and properly positioned.

I am sure Botham must regard himself as a shock bowler, and England must use him as such. There is no shortage of stock medium pacers. His captain needs to tell him, 'Come on, fire it. You have got to bowl quick.'

England's lack of bowling aggression was made all too clear in the Lord's Test against Pakistan in 1982. Without Willis there was no bite, and David Gower, the acting captain, should have reminded Botham that he had taken Bob's place. Instead Ian had bowled no more than three balls when, walking back to his mark, he put his hand about three inches high to indicate to the ground staff there was no bounce in the wicket. There was, however, no lack of bounce when Imran Khan ran in! If Botham had bowled quicker at the start Pakistan might not have had it all their own way. I could not imagine Brearley accepting the position as Gower did. But such a comparison is unfair.

Barring Sir Don Bradman, I doubt if any cricketer has had as much publicity on and off the field as Ian. Some he has brought on himself, and most people go through phases. Freddie Trueman did. Nowadays it is impossible for the sporting star to escape headlines – the bigger the name, the bigger the stories – it is the stark penalty of fame. I suppose the big-name sportsman has to accept it as part and parcel of his life and adapt himself accordingly. The wraps are never going to be put around Ian, that's for certain; he is the sort of lusty man some are going to take on in any case. If he'd lived in the wild west he would have been the fastest gun. I think Ian has to realise he's a target man, and now and again he's got to hold back and bite his tongue.

I shudder to think what English cricket would be like without him. Speaking as an old pro, who by modern standards didn't take much out of the game, I don't begrudge a penny of the fabulous money he is reputed to earn. If his income was doubled or trebled, it would not be too much. Consider his loyalty to the establishment. What would Packer not have done to recruit him? What could he command from an unofficial visit to South Africa? – for he is the plum they yearn to pluck. I heard a sum mentioned, which I know to be accurate, for one appearance in South Africa, which took the breath away.

Botham will always be identified with Brearley, who has left the game with a reputation few of the famous leaders of the past can equal. Unfortunately I never played under him, but studying his methods and the response of the teams he has led there can be no doubt that he was one of the great man-managers of cricket. The proof lies in his remarkable achievements with relatively poor sides. Normally a leader of a bad team sinks with his team. Captains like Stuart Surridge, Brian Sellers and Walter Robins at county level had outstanding teams. Look at the bowling Len Hutton had at his command in Australia – Frank Tyson, Brian Stratham, Trevor

Bailey, Bob Appleyard, Johnny Wardle and Alec Bedser –
and other victorious teams, and compare them with the resources available to Brearley. Take away Botham and Willis
and he scarcely had a great player with him in 1981.

Brearley is a captain on his own, and an exception to the
general rule that even the best of captains cannot make a poor
side into a good one. As a batsman Brearley was at least half
a class short of being Test standard. In the course of sixty-six
innings he never managed a century, and though he made
some useful scores he passed through some depressing runs
which were as worrying to the selectors as to the player
himself.

Keith Miller once made the perceptive observation that,
while Brearley's batting might not match up to Test levels,
his ability as a captain to get the maximum effort from every
member of the side, and his often brilliant catching close to
the wicket, elevated him to the rank of an all-rounder.

I suppose Brearley's luck was to lead at a time when there
were no Bradmans in sight, but he did all that was required
of him, and much more. Basically he made teams tick because
he earned their respect as a man of deep sympathy, understanding and intelligence.

So many young players disappoint me. They get so far,
and either stop or even go back. David Gower is the one
batsman with a natural flair and a beautiful style. In full flight
he is superb, and has an uncanny sense of timing, but his sort
of player – and I suppose I was also a stylist – tends to look
bad if he misses one and the off stump goes out of the ground.
Everyone says, 'What a casual shot.' But it isn't – it is the
way he plays.

The one criticism I would level at David is that he is
inclined to play those eye-catching shots square of the wicket
too early in an innings. I would rather he kept them under
check until he had 50 on the board. Instead of getting his
back foot across and hitting with an upright bat, he is inclined
to fall away and the stroke is uncontrolled and rushed. At
times he also falls away and fails to get over the ball when off

driving, and, as a result, it leaves the ground. For all that David is gloriously talented and has a fine record. Wally Hammond had not even started his Test career by the age Gower was when already established for England, and, in that sense, David is really only a beginner. Happily, by the tour to Australia in 1982-3 he began to reveal his true worth and he is the big hope for the future.

Phil Edmonds is the one player to baffle me. He is a highly intelligent man, until he gets on to a cricket field. All his problems, by which I mean missing out on tours and the Middlesex captaincy, and the mixed reactions to him among his fellow players, are upstairs. If I had his ability and background – he was captain of Cambridge in 1973 – I would throw away that floppy sun hat, concentrate on bowling on the line of the off stump, and stop the chat, much of which is amiable argument. Whatever the reasons it made no sense for Edmonds to be left behind while England sent three off-spinners to Australia in 1982-3.

15
An Over-Heated Game

Though I had worrying moments and sometimes looked forward to a rest towards the end of a hard season, I can honestly say I did not share Barry Richards' jaundiced view of the game. To me, cricket was (and still is!) a way of life, and as much a hobby as a living. Financially my earnings were modest, starting at four pounds a week and rising to £1,800 in the 1970 season with Worcestershire. Test matches and overseas tours brought honour, travel and sights I would never have otherwise experienced, but they were scarcely a financial bonanza. My two benefits produced £5,000 from Gloucestershire, and £7,500 from Worcestershire, which, compared with today's figures, even as the politicians say 'in real terms', did not exactly set me up for life. Important as it was in raising a family, money was not paramount in my thoughts. The moment players stop enjoying the game and regard it merely as a means to a living, first-class cricket is condemned to becoming a very stale affair.

The professional cricketer is better off financially, certainly at the top. Benefits have rocketed. Before the introduction of a minimum wage in 1978, the total earnings of county staffs amounted to £700,000. By 1982, the figure had risen to £1.5 million, not including money paid into pension schemes. The Cricketers Association, representing the players, has co-operated with the authorities because they realised all were in it together. Splendid – I am not envious. There is every incentive to carry on playing, particularly if they are fitter, as they claim they are, and remain in a high income bracket. There is also a pensions scheme.

I wonder, however, how long the present tax-free benefit system will continue. As I see it, there will have to be a central pool, as we have at present the strange situation of county clubs competing for cash with their beneficiaries. There have been too many instances of counties reporting a huge working loss in the same year as one of the players has hit the jackpot.

Nowadays the players have been given a lot of advantages, ranging from financial rewards to being able to take wives on tour, but I am not quite sure all the changes have been for the better. I can well understand Barry Richards or any other glamorous 'import' finding it hard to adjust to the county system which we were brought up in. The early discipline was particularly valuable to a young player, and helped to keep his feet firmly on the ground. The old custom of a senior looking after a junior, making certain he understood etiquettes and conventions and took care of his appearance, was always appreciated in retrospect and, along with county loyalty, formed the foundation of the professional game. Of course all that is regarded as very old hat now.

The older players were certainly conscious of their seniority. As the junior, I remember being responsible for the removal of the baggage from Cheltenham to the next game at Dover. Play ended at Cheltenham at 6.30 p.m. and, when the team arrived at Paddington, the rest grabbed their overnight bags and left me with the job of transporting the cricket kit down the long platform (with the aid of a trolley) and across London in two taxi cabs. I reached Dover at 4.30 a.m. and, within one over, I was at the wicket to help Charlie Barnett start a second-wicket stand of 181. My contribution was 73. We then fielded while Kent made 434 and Les Ames 212.

Far from there being 'no tactical team meetings' in those days, as a manager once said when advancing the claim that current players and teams have a far more advanced professional outlook, there were non-stop meetings – informal, maybe, but effective none the less. We would end the day over a few pints of ale and talk cricket. Inevitably the chief topic of discussion centred in the current game, and individual performances were analysed. Nowadays, as likely as not, players are off and away in their sponsored cars. (It is a sobering thought that the present itinerary of county matches, cup-ties and the John Player League would not be possible without motorways.)

I am sure that teams benefitted from being together and travelling together, and that cricket was better for the discipline, both on the field and in the dressing-room. Test matches were hard and tough, and the players would not have had it otherwise, but the cricket was played in a good spirit, and outbreaks of bad temper were rare.

Unhappily, that discipline is now lacking, and the record of violence and abuse, both on and off the field, steadily deteriorates. The game now accepts with resigned exasperation incidents which once shocked, and the cricket-lover is angered by the growing band of prima donnas who, because of the ineptitude of authority, seem to get away with anything. Wickets have been kicked down, umpires abused – even publicly by a captain and team management in the middle of Tests – bats thrown and opponents kicked in scenes which make my outburst of temper at Port-of-Spain seem absurdly trivial by comparison.

Some incidents involving famous players have not only besmirched the name of cricket but set an appalling example. I cannot believe the offenders would want their sons to play in the same way. What has got into the Australians I cannot guess. To bowl an under-arm along the ground to prevent New Zealand having the chance to score a six off the last ball of a one-day international was beyond belief. At one time the attitude would have been, 'If they can slog and win, good luck to them.' Surely money has not corrupted cricket to the extent that teams will stop at nothing to win?

Cricket is fast losing its unique tradition of fair play. Indeed the stage may have passed when the proud old phrase 'it isn't cricket' has any meaning. What was best in the game has been killed off by extreme nationalism which sees defeat as a disgrace, big money prizes, calculated gamesmanship (a posh veneer for cheating), the growth of so-called sledging (the practice of violent abuse of an opponent), and incessant appealing to make the life of an umpire miserable.

In a welter of indiscipline and collapsing standards, it is not possible for the various Boards of Control and the International Cricket Conference to escape censure. Frankly I believe that if all the national ruling bodies had been as conscientious as England's Test and County Cricket Board there would have been a different story. However, much as it goes against the grain for an old player to say so, it basically comes down to the attitude of the players and, sad to relate, of the captains, who have a duty to lead and set an example. Captains are failing in their essential duties.

In recent years few series have escaped some form of misbehaviour on the field, much of which has been absolutely appalling. Incidents have been too often and too well documented to give chapter and verse here, but I feel obliged to name Australia and Pakistan as particular offenders. As a bowler in a class of his own, a dedicated competitor and a man courageous enough by sheer will-power to defeat an injury threatening his career, Dennis Lillee has deservedly won universal admiration. But his reputation for being in the thick of controversy on the field is another side of him. To the watching cricket world it has seemed that he has been able to get away with anything because Australia are determined to play him in their team, come what may.

Captains have much to answer for. I am certain in my own mind that Lillee would not have had such a free rein if Greg Chappell had been captain; or, for that matter, had he played under the likes of Don Bradman, Lindsay Hassett, Richie Benaud, Bobby Simpson or Bill Lawry, who were all, in their different ways, tough but very fair.

If, however, control is beyond the captain of the day, it behoves the governing body jealously to guard standards. At the moment, it has to be said, confidence is beginning to wane. Not many stones can be cast in England's direction. I wonder how many Boards would have imposed a three-year Test ban, thereby seriously weakening the national side, as the TCCB did after the unofficial tour of South Africa in 1981-2. Whatever the arguments over the justness, or otherwise, of the decision, the Board upheld a principle as they saw it. They should be commended, not criticised, for their actions.

Like all old players and cricket-lovers I was shocked at the events at Perth in 1982, when Terry Alderman had to retire from the match after grappling with over-excited drunks who had run on to the field. How much a regrettable television commercial shown in Australia was to blame one can only guess, but to my mind cricket, and Anglo-Australian relations in particular, have reached a sorry state if provocative publicity is needed to whip up interest. The so-called marketing of the game was part of the Australian Board's deal with Kerry Packer, and the film purported to show Englishmen denigrating Australia's chances. Every comment was made against a background of familiar English landmarks and in a traditional pub and, if the interviewees were English and their comments unrehearsed, I would be surprised.

Would many Englishmen really say: 'Chappell had so many ducks that he could open a farm', or that Lillee was 'over the top'? The answer is possibly: only if they were paid to do so.

I thought the film was in deplorable taste and took the ancient rivalry a stage further into aggression. The question needed to be asked: who is in charge of Australian cricket, the Board, or the BPL organisation, who are selling the game for the Board? The film could only cause aggro and bad feeling. One Australian journalist who rang me from the London bureau to get my views, remarked, 'Well I think it is quite clever.' Probably it was in its own way, but the spirit of the film was a negation of the true interests of cricket. Clever people do not leap over fences and rush on to the field and grapple with players.

E.W. Swanton hit on the right words when he described the Australian cricket public as more fickle and aggressively jingoistic than the English. Visiting teams are accustomed to being 'rubbished', and the old cry of 'wingeing Poms' is soon in evidence, but there is one new development that I find particularly disagreeable. Even before the one-day finals between Australia and New Zealand in 1983, Kim Hughes, the Australian captain, was saying that Glenn Turner played only one-day cricket (his last full Test had been in 1977) because the ball 'never rises more than half stump high.'

John Woodcock said in *The Times* that the comment was both 'offensive and stupid', and pointed out that Turner was one of only three non-English batsmen, together with Bradman and Zaheer Abbas, to have scored a hundred first-class centuries.

Turner's reply was that batting against Australians was a matter of being subjected to constant abuse. Back home, he said that he felt a measure of relief. 'When you come back from there you almost feel like you've been in Vietnam', he added, with a touch of colourful exaggeration.

I know Turner well and, if I had the choice between him and Hughes purely as batsmen, my decision would be made in one second flat. I also recognise that modern captains are absolutely bang in the front line of media exposure. They are constantly interviewed and, in the interests of publicity, expected to give quotes to all and sundry. The modern captain, therefore, must not let slip unguarded words. I cannot imagine what came over Hughes – perhaps he felt obliged to live up to the tough guy image.

Cricket had come to a pretty pass when Turner was quoted as saying, 'What pleased me was that, as the tour went along, I got more and more boos as I went out to bat. That meant I must have been doing all right.' Against that I have to contrast my own experiences as an English player in Australia. Play was hard, the crowds critical, and the barracking fairly evenly distributed, but there was always generous appreciation for a good performance. Sir Frankie Worrell's side of 1960–61 were given an emotional farewell as they rode in open cars through the Melbourne streets. Has that fair dinkum spirit died in such a short space of time? Must the Aussie public have villains to boo as well as heroes to cheer? (The unrelenting campaign against Mike Brearley on his last tour is hard to forget.) And do they really fall for those dreadful television commercials, with slogans like 'the hottest cricket in a hundred summers', or am I getting out of date?

A difficult position has come about in Australia, it must be said, because it is evident that a lot of the cricket is run by a commercial television station. There are now conflicting interests. Not to put too fine a point on it, television companies are concerned mainly with selling advertising space – the purpose of their existence – and it is an unhappy fact if public interest has to be stimulated by intense rivalry, aggro and the like. At one time there would have been no need for well-oiled publicity machines to go into action to persuade spectators to flock in their tens of thousands to the Test grounds when the Ashes were at stake.

Almost a million watched the five Tests in 1936–7, including 350,534 for one match at Melbourne, and there were 90,800 just for one day in the West Indies series of 1960–61. There was certainly no need for spoofing up commercials to induce spectators to watch Bradman and Hammond bat, or Lindwall and Miller bowl.

Hutton fended off an aggressive radio interviewer before a Test at Brisbane with words the present-day promoters might note: 'We're only going to play a cricket match, not starting a war with machine-guns.'

Sport and the media have double standards and fall deep into the pit of hypocrisy. There is a lot of editorial tut-tutting when Dennis Lillee or John McEnroe boils over, but the fact is that incidents make good television, titillating reading, and bring in more cash customers through the gate. Everybody jumps in, quick to condemn, and is equally quick to savour the event.

In cricket a lot of the trouble has its origins in the new excitability which has swept through teams, with players leaping around as if their pants were on fire, constant and frantic appealing, and absurd bouts of self-congratulation at the fall of a wicket. I cringe when I see some of the celebrations after the dismissal of an ordinary batsman. I wonder what would have followed if the same carry-on had been prevalent in the days of Bradman, the three W's, Hutton, Compton, May and the rest. At the Melbourne centenary Test, Harold Larwood, a witness to some hysteria of this kind, asked, 'What the hell's going on?' Indeed, what *is* going on?

In a Nat West cup-tie I saw a wicket-keeper get hugs, pats on the back and handshakes for his part in a run-out so simple that most grannies could have done it equally well. By contrast, I was recently watching an old clip of Freddie Trueman taking his 300th Test wicket, an excuse if ever there was one for a bout of jubilation and self-congratulation. Neil Hawke, the 'victim', shook Freddie's hand as he went on his way to the pavilion, and then the England players offered their handshakes. No hysterical leaps in the air and hugging and kissing, which now follows the fall of every wicket. I hesitate to think what might happen now to celebrate a bowler's 300th Test wicket, or the dismissal of Don Bradman or Wally Hammond. Modern players tell me they are more emotional than players were in my day and are under more pressure: an interesting theory, but I think they are just psyching themselves, and the indiscipline is communicated to some of the more impressionable spectators.

Ian Chappell and, to a lesser extent, Tony Greig were in the vanguard of captains who created an aggressive atmosphere. I say this as a good mate of Ian, whose many qualities include intense loyalty to his friends. He and Greig, in my opinion, overdid it. In the 1974–5 series, until he was stopped by his manager Alec Bedser, Greig began pointing to the pavilion whenever an Australian was dismissed. To prove that a bad habit dies hard, Robin Jackman repeated the gesture against Pakistan in England in 1982.

Sometimes the new-style aggression becomes counter-productive. Colin Cowdrey told me of his first innings at Perth when he flew to Australia in an emergency to join Mike Denness' injury-stricken side. He had to go straight into a Test, and had got over the hard part, with Lillee coming to the end of his spell, when a wicket fell. Greig came in and hit the first ball from Lillee head-high through the covers with a flat bat, and was signalling a four before the ball reached the boundary.

At once Lillee was two yards quicker and, instead of coming off, he bowled an extra four overs! Whenever I played, my golden rule was never to argue with fast bowlers and umpires!

16
Cricket at the Crossroads

In the course of time I fear the last two decades or so are likely to be remembered more for follies than for wise administration: the often reckless self-interest of counties in lowering the drawbridge to an invading army of overseas players, the changed values stemming from one-day competitions, and the emancipation of the players – better known as player power. The gap between the three-day championship and Test cricket widened to a veritable chasm, which made the selection of England teams and touring parties increasingly difficult. Players of genuine class became rarer – indeed, in bleaker moments, they seemed an endangered species.

Some extraordinarily silly rules and regulations, notably bonus points and the restriction of first innings to a maximum of 100 overs – surely the most inane of all – lowered standards and the credibility of the championship, on which the true strength of English cricket rests and must be judged. At one time even the follow-on was forbidden. I played in a match when Worcestershire, having declared at 520 for 3 and dismissed Somerset for 270, were put in the ludicrous position of having to bat a second time! As it happened, Worcestershire won by 264 runs, but there was no knowing what freakish interventions were possible – even the remote possibility of Somerset fighting back, after a generous declaration, and having a go at Worcestershire in the end.

I firmly believe that cricket, already a complex game,

should be kept as simple as possible, and that the more artificial regulations are introduced, the less appealing it becomes. The last things the average spectator needs are complications.

To me the whole point is to win fairly and squarely without the alleged incentives of bonus points, and I am in favour of four-day championship matches with a minimum number of overs to be completed in a day's play. There must be two sound arguments for its introduction; one, the better to prepare players for five-day Tests and improve all-round standards; two, to make it a real championship, with each side meeting all the other counties once. There has to be a stipulated number of overs, because unfortunately the players cannot be trusted to maintain a reasonable over rate, and it banishes any threat of four-day games becoming unduly slow. All right, perhaps have a bonus point for a first innings lead, but even that is questionable. If a side cannot win in four days, it hardly deserves a compensatory award.

A really serious competition, bereft of gimmicks, is necessary if the players are to rediscover old skills and techniques, and to teach batsmen to play longer innings, which is a matter of disciplined concentration and a state of mind. A lack of mental stamina was painfully evident during Bob Willis' tour of Australia in 1982–3, when, astonishingly, only Derek Randall and David Gower scored centuries, though 108 innings were played by England batsmen in five Tests. There was no lack of scores between 50 and 80, but that, in the context of Test cricket, is not good enough – a job only half done. If that sounds like a harsh assessment, I would say it is merely an indictment of the acceptance of lower standards.

I know I am going back to the dark ages in the eyes of some young batsmen of today, but it is an inescapable fact that when Sir Len Hutton, Denis Compton, Peter May and the other leading batsmen of their day, reached 50, the next target was a second 50, and after that fresh guard was taken as if the innings was only just starting.

Denis Compton tells of a blast from his captain Wally

Hammond when exuberance got the better of him after scoring a century in his first Test against Australia at Trent Bridge. He was twenty years old at the time and England had already scored more runs than seems possible in these days, but, instead of the expected praise, Compton was severely admonished by Hammond. 'Don't you ever do that to me again,' he said. 'You will remember, I hope, that when you play against Australia and you make a hundred, you take fresh guard, start again and rub it in.' Heaven knows what Hammond would have to say to those who all too often get out on the wrong side of a century, having got over the most difficult part of an innings. And, please don't tell me that modern bowling, field placing and pressures are more difficult to cope with.

For my own part, if I got out other than to a good ball which would have defeated me at any stage of an innings, I was furious with myself; and I expected, and fully deserved, a rocket from the captain. Places in England's Test side are too easily held these days.

Surely it ought not to be beyond the wit of man, or the computer, to devise a championship programme of sixteen four-day matches for each county, to be played during midweek, when attendances are at their lowest. Weekends could then be reserved for the single innings competitions. I would go further and explore the possibility of putting aside some weeks exclusively for Test matches. They already hog the scene, as it is, devouring all the time on television and radio and all the space in newspapers, and also take away the leading players. If a clash could be avoided, the championship would be immeasurably stronger and be given a fresh status without taking anything away from the Test series. The county championship and five-day games are as necessary as the one-day fiestas; but they demand separate techniques and attitudes, and the danger, as I see it, is of the one-day mentality and approach taking over. In my opinion English cricket standards will not return unless there is a proper training ground for Tests – and that must be the championship – and unless the number of overseas players is substantially reduced.

Another cause of decline can be traced back to the lush condition of the outfields, which, nourished by fertilisers, tends to keep the shine on the ball; this, in turn, encourages the use of the medium pace bowler, who, with one or two distinguished exceptions, is absolutely useless at Test level, particularly abroad. The difference that conditions make can be startling and is a constant trap for selectors. Bowlers who are outstanding in England can be flops when they are taken away from pitches producing movement off the seam. Ken Higgs provided a good example. In the 1966 series I stood in the slips and saw Ken create all sorts of problems for batsmen of the class of Sir Gary Sobers, Seymour Nurse, Basil Butcher, Rohan Kanhai and Conrad Hunte. He got the first wicket in each of the first West Indies innings, and finished with twenty-four wickets. The only other bowler to go into double figures was John Snow, with half that number. Yet in Australia in 1965–6 Higgs' two wickets in his one Test cost 51.00 runs each.

I have vivid memories of the Australian Alan Connolly still swinging the ball after seventy-five overs when Headingley had a very green outfield for the Test of 1968; in fact when the new ball was taken it swung nothing like the old one.

Obviously some balls swing more than others, and react if there is humidity or a cloud cover – and I am somewhat bemused when learned professors occasionally say there is scientific proof that the ball does not swing – but as a general rule I have no doubt there is more movement if the outfield is strongly grassed. I am sure it has been a contributory factor to failing standards. When I first went to The Oval with Gloucestershire, the shine would be off within eight overs and, unless the bowler had genuine pace, accuracy, the rare skill of Alec Bedser, or gave the ball a definite tweak, he stood little chance.

So much hinges on pitches. They must have pace. Without it, cricket becomes humdrum and strictly for the mediocre.

Unhappily, mediocrity has become the accepted norm, and recently spectators have been starved all too often of the highest arts of the game. The sight of Ray Lindwall, Wes Hall, Freddie Trueman, Jim Laker and the other bowling greats running up to the wicket was comparable to the fluency of the master batsmen. But I am afraid the contrast of an ordinary batsman collecting a century against ordinary bowlers using the same methods is unattractive enough to turn spectators away from the grounds.

Since my retirement the changes have been so sweeping that when I look at the scene, both at international and domestic level, I begin to wonder if I was ever part of it. I am frequently told by well-meaning friends, looking at today's rewards, that I played in the wrong period. I am far from convinced of that, even if we were paupers by today's standards. The way the Kerry Packer enterprise was set up, the clandestine meetings during the Melbourne Centenary Test, the silly subterfuges and cloak-and-dagger methods to get in and out of South Africa on money-making unofficial Tests are not activities which appeal to me. The unwelcome finger of politics has prodded every sporting corner, all-powerful players rule the roost, and there is an increasing danger of a calamitous split between white and non-white countries. Double standards abound as politicians, still happy to trade together, quarrel like alley cats over sport. What a tragedy it is that world leaders cannot get along together, as cricketers of all shades, creeds and cultures are able to do.

Huge cheques for a few months' work, even at the cost of some aggro, are, however, a temptation even to the most highly principled player. Some of the arguments for going to Packer and South Africa can be dismissed as unworthy of consideration. If on the other hand there was an honest admission that the cheque was paying off the mortgage, going on school fees and the like, I would understand. I would also admit that at certain stages of my career I would have given an offer from Packer the most serious consideration. Had it come when I had my row with Gloucestershire, at the age of thirty-five or after my Test ban towards the end of my playing days, I would have gone to the World Series. But at other stages, and in other moods, I think I would have held back and regarded my career and reputation as too precious to be damaged.

For all I know the money might have been worth it, but the Kent trio of Alan Knott, Derek Underwood and Bob Woolmer were never the same as far as England were concerned, even if Knott helped to beat Australia in 1981. Underwood remained the best left-arm bowler in the country, and he would have meant a lot to England if he had gone to Australia in 1982–3. If nothing else he would have been accurate. The leading so-called rebels to South Africa, under Graham Gooch, showed a lack of business sense and gumption.

Gooch, Geoff Boycott and John Emburey were England regulars, and Les Taylor, Wayne Larkins and Peter Willey were on the verge of the team. They must have known they risked a ban, and the likelihood of missing Australia, with all the perks to be had on top of a big basic fee – some estimates put the grand total to be upwards of £30,000 – and at the same time putting themselves out of commercial reckoning for the three years they were not available for England. During that time no ad-man was going to say, 'Let's get Gooch for a commercial.' The other aspect – a measure of public condemnation – might not, in these materialistic days, be held to be so important. Yet I still think that one's personal standing is not something to be lightly tossed away.

Those seeking to preserve the best of the traditions, and wanting cricket to hold on to its reputation as a 'gentleman's game', have not had much encouragement in recent years. All old hat, some may say, but it will be a sad state of affairs, bringing no end of problems in its wake, including lack of sponsorship and membership support, if control from the top is not tightened up, and if the players, who have gained almost every concession they have sought, become bigger than the game. The considerable danger lies in their taking more out of the game than they put in to it and of agents, accountants and all the 'fringe' people cynically exploiting the good-will built up over the years.

Reforms must begin right at the top with the International Cricket Conference, which, in my opinion, has a poor track record. An enormous clanger was dropped in 1982 when the Conference refused even to meet the South African delegation. No doubt the blame was to be laid at the feet of some governments, whose control embraces cricket, but the fact was that from then onwards South Africa set up an elaborate structure, backed by Government funds, to bypass the Conference. At the moment the players have more influence to shape the future of the game, which cannot be right.

In our own domestic structure the qualification rules have got to be tightened up to make it less easy to move around. The counties have got to be the bosses. In Australia cricket now seems to be controlled less by the Australian Board than by the Packer organisation for commercial television. On the whole I think the game was cheapened by Australia's television war. Little things irked me when I watched the 1982-3 series, like that stupid duck which was flashed on the screen when a batsman was out without scoring. If contrived capers, coloured clothing, white balls and the rest represent the game's progress and is the pattern for the future, I cannot believe too many of my playing contemporaries are sorry at having missed out. Furthermore I hope and trust it will be an unexportable Australian product.

On the question of umpiring I find myself firmly among the establishment ranks, if only because I fear the popular cures of so-called neutrals, electronic aids or a third official on the field would, in the end, be worse than the complaint. Frankly, I never went on a tour, winning or losing, without coming across umpiring problems of one sort or another, and no matter how well briefed beforehand, even the most disciplined team can be upset by contentious decisions; others do manage to accept it stoically as an occupational hazard, but cricket needs to concern itself with the growing practice of pressurising umpires by incessant and cynical appealing. Pakistan reached the depths in England in 1982. As a batsman I deplored shouts from all directions for leg-before, when in all reasonableness only the bowler and wicket-keeper were in a position to make a fair appeal.

As more money has come into cricket, and the accent has been on winning at all costs, appealing has become wilder, more hysterical and without conscience. Not only has the judgement of umpires been called into question, but even their impartiality. Basically I found umpires everywhere, irrespective of standards, to be honest and trying hard to give of their best and to make as few mistakes as is humanly possible. Genuine errors will always be made and must be tolerated, but there is one area of umpiring which is dishonest and intolerable.

I refer to compensatory decisions – that is, giving a batsman out merely to amend an earlier mistake. Rather than righting an injustice, it is, in fact, making two mistakes. Nor can mistakes level out by the end of a match or a series, for it depends when, and at what situation, in a match the mistake is made. When, for instance, John Dyson was clearly run out, as proved by television, in the first over of the Sydney Test in 1983, Australia not only had a bonus of 79 runs, but a second crucial chance to build a foundation for the innings. To my way of thinking, even a favourable decision at a later stage does not put the balance even. Undoubtedly Australia were the better side, but there was a deal of sympathy for England from those who followed the series on television.

Test match umpiring standards might fall disappointingly below the hoped-for standards – and, while England seemed to be getting the worst of it in Australia, India bitterly complained in Pakistan – I can see no logical alternative to trusting the officials. While it is true that other sports, like both codes of football, have neutrals, and cricket's officials are, apart from England, amateurs in a highly professional game, an élite Test panel drawn from all countries would not be practical or workable.

I reckon for a start that ten out of twelve would be English, which would be resented by the rest of the cricket world, and in this sensitive age there would inevitably be outrage, if, say, there wasn't a West Indian or a Sri Lankan on the panel. To pander to national sensitivities and to get 'fair' representation would at once diminish the overall standard and defeat the main objective.

The time has come to help umpires. For a start captains should not be allowed to pass judgements in public. There is a procedure to follow if a complaint is felt justified. Captains must assert their authority and stamp out bad and aggressive appealing, and the abuse of opponents – another growth industry. Authority must not shrink from its clear duty to back captains all the way, even if it means unpopular decisions and temporary bans for key players.

I also suggest that the grossly over-burdened umpires should be relieved of the responsibility of decision-making in the often contentious matter of the fitness of a ground – an opinion I held long before the disgraceful scenes at Lord's during the Cornhill Centenary Test when, incredible to relate, 'Dicky' Bird and David Constant had to be given a police escort through the Long Room.

Let them umpire the cricket match, and pass on the onus of starting, or resuming, play to another authority, be it the managers of the teams or a neutral observer. As the managers have a vested interest and could employ a little gamesmanship, a neutral is probably the ideal solution. The same authority should also be empowered to give instant punishments for indiscipline or behaviour calculated to bring the game into disrepute.

The mere presence of an official with overall disciplinary powers might cool some of the hot-heads, who, sadly, have been getting away with it too long.

Better late than never, but it is now at last being recognised that umpires, too, have their feelings and need to prepare for a big occasion just as much as the players, who are not on the field from the first ball to the last, as umpires are. The amount of concentration required by an umpire over five days is severely demanding. I had an interesting insight into an umpire's approach when I ran into Barry Meyer, the Test umpire and a former Gloucestershire colleague, while on holiday in Spain after the 1982 season. Meyer, it will be recalled, came in as a late substitute for David Constant after an objection by India for some reason best known to themselves, for the Lord's Test.

By his own admission Barry has had better matches, and he assured me that, given a mere twenty-four hours notice, he just was not mentally prepared to stand in a Test. I could understand his reaction, as I, in common with every player, had to readjust myself and my thoughts before playing for my country. We all tend to take umpires for granted, forgetting they 'lose the toss' every day and have to take the field until the close of play. Legislators have tended to pass the buck on to umpires in so many ways. I am sure that one way to bring about better umpiring is to reduce their area of responsibility to adjudicating the actual play.

I think it will always have to be accepted that the standard of umpiring is bound to vary, like the play itself. There always will be vintage and non-vintage eras of both players and umpires – strong umpires and weak umpires. Players are now much more difficult to handle, and less receptive to discipline. Umpires are less likely to get the help they used to have from players on borderline decisions, and the chivalry of 'walking' is on the way out. In short the umpire's lot, like a policeman's, is not a happy one. The excellent idea of having overseas umpires for a season in the championship unfortunately did not work out, and it is regrettable that outside England more old players do not take up the profession.

One of the snags in Australia, where I found umpires usually went exactly by the book, is that a retired player would have to start at the bottom in the fifth grade. I met with the same uninviting prospect when, years ago, I applied for a coaching certificate and was told I would have to start from the beginning. To go through the basics of stance, grip, backlift and the like was a bit too much for me – I doubt if any two players are exactly alike in any case – and I passed it over. Umpiring and coaching have much in common, in that a distinguished playing background is not an absolute necessity, but I feel umpires need playing experience to have a feel for the game, for this, in turn, develops an instinct to make the right decision. No amount of theory can make up for a lack of practical experience.

A lot of cricket's current problems would disappear with strong and purposeful captaincy, and I am bound to think the appointment of county team managers might also be considered superfluous. The fact is that if a county has a good captain it does not need a manager. When I was captain of Gloucestershire, and then Worcestershire, I am sure the presence of a manager in the dressing-room could not have been tolerated for long, even if he had been my best friend. The overlapping duties must clash and, as I see it, no captain worth his salt is going to be tactically influenced by a manager. Out on the field, where it counts, only the captain can be in absolute command.

Having said that, I am sure there is a place for the county manager, as distinct from the first-team boss. Micky Stewart immediately springs to mind as outstanding, which casts no aspersions on the qualities of the captain, Roger Knight, but recognises the extension of Micky's duties as an organiser of cricket within the whole county. I imagine that for him, like Ray Illingworth and others, the winter is the busiest time. Stewart spends a lot of time with the Second XI, colts and so on, as well as coaching in winter, but he also had the advantage of returning to The Oval virtually as a stranger to the county players. I think that is essential, for any manager who plays alongside members of the playing staff is grossly handicapped.

Illingworth won my admiration for his bravery in not only tackling a situation at Yorkshire, on and off the field, which has the rest of the counties looking on in bemused regret, but taking on the captaincy at the age of fifty. That is what I would regard as gallantry beyond the call of duty.

Even if cricket is wise and bold enough to take all the right measures, it will take time and patience to restore standards eroded by a decade of muddle and conflicting loyalties. I understand the argument of counties who proclaim their first duty is to their members and local public and go out with a chequebook and sign an overseas star. I also understand the legitimate complaint of selectors who have an ever narrowing field of talent from which to choose (imagine in 1983 dropping the likes of Ken Barrington and Geoff Boycott for slow play!). Short-term policies have led to a long-term run-down of playing resources, and half-prepared players are rushed into the Test side. Nobody should be surprised when they fail to come up to expectations. I must admit to blinking at some of the batting and bowling performances I saw on television from Australia in 1982-3. England were so unprofessional.

I look around at the modern facilities, like indoor schools, and listen to the enthusiastic talk of the coaches, and I wonder where it has gone wrong. Too much one-day cricket at all levels – yes; monkeying around with the conditions of play in the championship – yes; some deterioration in the preparation of the pitches – yes; different outlooks and interests, including a swing to the games and pastimes of individual participation – again, yes, to a degree.

In 1968 the National Cricket Association, backed by the Test and County Cricket Board, MCC, various sponsors and devoted officials, was set up to advance the game below first-class level. Some said it was fifty years too late, but it is better to be late than never, and there are now six NCA coaches, headed by Keith Andrew, who is based at Lord's. They, and the English Schools Cricket Association, perform wonders, but sometimes it is an uphill fight.

Too many schools do not have cricket on the sporting syllabus, for two reasons. Firstly, pitches and facilities are either not available or nor up to scratch. Secondly, it is far easier to set boys to run around a field, or to play football the whole year round. Astonishingly some of the leading physical education colleges, Loughborough included, do not have cricket on the curriculum as a compulsory subject. The result must be that countless sports masters have been appointed with little or no knowledge of cricket, and an extra burden is placed on the growing number of national coaches. Nor is there any justification for teaching softball or rounders in preference to cricket, if only because the chances of continuing those activities after school leaving age are remote.

It is sad that in a vast area like Lancashire only four comprehensive schools are playing an acceptable class of cricket, and in Northumberland, an area running from the Tyne to the Tweed, fifteen of the forty-four comprehensives have given up the game. Yet a questionnaire circulated to forty-eight secondary schools in London, which produced thirty-four replies, showed that, with all age groups, cricket was the most popular summer game. The causes for concern were that cricket was not compulsory at first and second year levels for eight schools, and a similar number had no connection with clubs, not even an old boys' side.

Fortunately the gap which used to exist between schools and clubs is being bridged. Many clubs now have a thriving colts section, and young players have opportunities, undreamt of in my youth, of touring abroad. Even junior Test matches are played. One two-yearly series between England and the West Indies is financed by Agatha Christie Ltd, whose chairman Mathew Pritchard is a cricket fanatic. Just before the death of the famous author, he persuaded her to leave money in trust for a project which has already helped to produce Test players for both countries. At national level, sponsored tournaments include an eight-a-side event for Under-13's, an Under-15 club competition, and an Under-16 county championship.

Another hopeful development is that more and more artificial pitches are being used, which produce a consistent bounce and remove the physical fear of playing on a bad surface. Hampshire, for example, have put down eighteen of them, which I see as a wise investment. These are steps in the right direction.

17
Doctor's Orders

I write, more in sorrow than anger, after the winter's disappointments in Australia. The defeats in New Zealand in the limited-over matches reflected the mood of a demoralised side, but I don't subscribe to the view that the modern tours are too long. The sixty-four thousand dollar question facing English cricket is straightforward: how can standards be restored? To my mind, as I have said, the first requirement is the introduction of a four-day championship in which the young players can develop better techniques in both batting and bowling and be better prepared for the tougher arena of Test matches. This would also help to instil the discipline and harder mental attitudes which are necessary.

Far from causing a disruption, four-day matches would lead to a better structured domestic programme, not to mention a fairer competition, with sixteen matches and with each county playing one game against every other county. The championship could occupy the weekdays, leaving the limited-over competitions to the week-ends when crowds are bigger. Also, with sixteen matches, it would be possible to leave the field clear for at least the first three Tests. In my view that would strengthen public interest in Tests and the England team, and also allow the clubs to see more of their star players.

The fact is that county games are virtually ignored during Tests – at least for three parts of the season. Unless a team is running for the title and there is special local interest, the average run-of-the-mill county fixture does not stand a ghost of a chance during a Test. Even the spectators ringing the boundary have ears tuned into transistors relaying the big occasion. The county match is scarcely worth the effort and expense. How much better it would be if Tests had the entire stage to themselves.

On the issue of overseas players I find myself adopting an increasingly nationalistic stance. If English cricket is to be jealous of its standards and be fair to itself, and to present and future generations, county cricket has to be an English game for English players. The era of foreign domination has to end, and counties must become self-reliant. The influx of imports has not only chipped away at the foundations of England's national side, but led to a blasé public. Once upon a time cricket followers anticipated with relish the arrival of touring teams and the big foreign names. The opening fixture at Worcester was a real occasion. Nowadays it is possible to see the world's leading performers any day in the week in county cricket. Familiarity has bred, if not contempt, a little indifference. Some of the magic, some of the curiosity value, has gone. Perhaps it was a sign of the times when one national newspaper did not even report the arrival of a recent Australian side to England. At one time that would have been unthinkable.

There is also another reason why it is in our own interests to stick to home-produced talent – the mundane but important matter of cash. In a difficult financial climate it seems to me to be rank folly to give fat contracts to outsiders while the gap between the top boys and the rank-and-file is ever widening. It may not be easy to eliminate cricket's globe-trotters, who play strictly for cash, but, in the end, it would prove to be the salvation of England's game if it was possible to do so. Counties need to be far-seeing, to stand on their own feet and look beyond their short-term interests.

I also firmly believe the time is long overdue to stop listening to others who tell us how to run our own cricket. The issue of apartheid in sport threatens the whole international structure. It is throttling cricket like a python coiled around its neck. Interference by governments of all political shades, and the pettiness of United Nations groups compiling so-called black lists, are growing daily. The smaller the government, the more parish-minded the ministers, the more the noise and meddlesome intrusion. And the interference is met by weak-kneed and irresolute defences in the pious hope that by doing nothing and remaining mute the problem will vanish in the night. It won't.

When Guyana threw down the gauntlet by deporting Robin Jackman – and with him the entire England side – it should have been picked up and answered by catching the first plane home. Guyana should have been left to face the wrath of the rest of the West Indies, and the catastrophic consequence of a ruined tour. Now the West Indies authorities have to deal with a challenge within their own cricketing ranks. Events are getting out of control, and unless some common sense is knocked into some uncommonly thick skulls an irreparable tragedy will befall the once innocent world of cricket.

Frankly, I would not care to be a politician anywhere – particularly in the West Indies – who becomes responsible for the end of Test cricket or its reduction to, at best, a series of matches between the same ethnic groups. Part of the charm and appeal of Test matches is, or at least used to be, the exhibition of skills and exuberance of the West Indies, the subtle spin-bowling of the Indians and the emergence of Pakistan as a power in their own right. How unutterably boring it would be for the West Indies, India, Pakistan and Sri Lanka to be locked in perpetual combat! Indeed, West Indies cricket would not survive, for its financial life depends on playing in Australia and England.

I welcome England's bid to curb the growth of unfair appealing. The orchestrated appeal designed to intimidate umpires is a menace and a disgrace. I hope the players respond, and I hope further that this will be the first step towards a clean-up and a restoration of the old accepted standards.

Cricket is too great a game to be sullied and brought to its knees by hot-headed players or pompous politicians. The rest should stick up for the things which earned the game its reputation. I believe that cricket is now at the crossroads, and I pray we shall take the right direction.

Index